PENGUIN CLASSICS

A HUNDRED MEASURES OF TIME

ARCHANA VENKATESAN is associate professor of Comparative Literature and Religious Studies at the University of California, Davis. She has received numerous grants, including fellowships from the National Endowment for the Arts, National Endowment for the Humanities, American Institute of Indian Studies and Fulbright. Her research interests are in the intersection of text and performance in south India, as well as in the translation of early and medieval Tamil poetry into English. She is the author of *The Secret Garland: Āṇṭāḷ's Tiruppāvai and Nācciyār Tirumoḻi* (2010), and is collaborating with Francis Clooney of Harvard University on an English translation of Nammāḻvār's *Tiruvāymoḻi*.

A HUNDRED MEASURES OF TIME TIRUVIRUTTAM

Nammāḻvār

Translated from the Tamil by
Archana Venkatesan

PENGUIN BOOKS
An imprint of Penguin Random House

PENGUIN BOOKS

USA | Canada | UK | Ireland | Australia
New Zealand | India | South Africa | China | Singapore

Penguin Books is part of the Penguin Random House group of companies whose addresses can be found at global.penguinrandomhouse.com

Published by Penguin Random House India Pvt. Ltd
4th Floor, Capital Tower 1, MG Road,
Gurugram 122 002, Haryana, India

Penguin Random House India

First published by Penguin Books India 2014

10 9 8 7 6 5 4 3 2

ISBN 9780143066378

Typeset in Bembo by Eleven Arts, Delhi
Printed at Repro India Limited

www.penguin.co.in

FSC www.fsc.org MIX Paper from responsible sources FSC® C047271

This is a legitimate digitally printed version of the book and therefore might not have certain extra finishing on the cover.

for my teachers

CONTENTS

ACKNOWLEDGEMENTS

This book began because of the largesse of the National Endowment for the Humanities. On the practical front, a fellowship in 2007–08 from this venerable institution supported a year of research in India. In a more abstract and not easily quantifiable way, the time away gave me much needed distance and afforded me a special opportunity to explore new pathways. One of these many paths—a road less travelled—led me in completely unanticipated directions that I am only now beginning to understand. For that I am deeply grateful, and my thanks to the NEH goes well beyond this book, the tangible fruits of that magical time in India.

Although I was a new addition, both the Departments of Comparative Literature and Religious Studies, University of California, Davis, released me from teaching and administrative responsibilities for the 2007–08 academic year. Since that time, I have been privileged to be a part of two wonderful and energetic programmes. The supportive environment combined with the path-breaking scholarship of my colleagues has done much to nurture my own intellectual curiosity.

The Oxford Centre for Hindu Studies and the Shivdasani Fellowship entered my life and the life of this book at a crucial stage. They provided a haven of retreat for my quarter of sabbatical between January and March 2013. If not for the generosity of the fellowship and the equal generosity of the staff of OCHS, this book would still remain a random collection of arbitrary, scattered files on my computer. They provided a space for quiet, thoughtful reflection that was instrumental in bringing this book to fruition. The vibrant life of the centre—seminars, lectures and informal discussions—have shaped the character of this book in ways both large and small. A thousand *pranam*s to Judit Bajusz, Anuradha Dooney, Gavin Flood, Jessica Frazier, Lal Krishna, Rembert Lutjherms, Shaunaka Rishi Das and Ken Valpey for their witty conversation, poetry readings and Kamadhenu-like kindness, and for creating a place that came to feel like home. A special thanks to the centre's own Annapurnas: Judit, Anu and Shyama who fed me, fed me, fed me, and to Shaunaka and Gavin for introducing me to Dosa Park.

The staff of the various Oxford libraries were the epitome of patience as I accumulated stacks of books over the course of my stay. In particular, thanks must go to the Sackler Library for allowing my books to occupy entire shelves. Although I wasn't a fellow of the college, the Harris Manchester College Library, Oxford, was quick to give me access to key sources in a timely manner. Thanks to Katrina Malone, Harris Manchester College, for her aid in securing Krishnaswami Aiyangar's *Early History of Vaishnavism in South India*. My thanks also go to Joanna Snelling of Corpus Christi College Library for all her able assistance in tracking down materials related to J.S.M. Hooper, and for finding a class photo from 1905 that allowed me finally to put a face to the man I had been researching.

Through RISA-L (the email list of Religion in South Asia Section), the virtual community of South Asia scholars, I was able to track down information on J.S.M. Hooper. Anita Ray, Will Sweetman and Arun Jones directed me to collections, libraries and sources that helped me flesh out how Hooper's translation, *Hymns of the Ālvārs*, came to be.

Over the years, the Annual UC Berkeley Tamil Conference has provided a safe and supportive venue to share some of my preliminary thinking on the *Tiruviruttam*, on Nammalvar and on Araiyar Cevai. George and Kausalya Hart have hosted this conference for almost a decade, and created a space of exciting intellectual exchange on all things Tamil. Every year, I eagerly looked forward to the annual *nalama* email from Kausalya that announces the conference's theme and invitees. Whether it was *palam* (bridge) or the Pantiyas, the Tamil conference never failed to stimulate discussion and new thinking. It was at one such conference that I met Crispin Branfoot and our mutual love of Pantiya Nadu has grown over several cups of coffee and enthusiastic discussions of Andal. Crispin—thank you for the lively Tuesday afternoon conversations in Oxford, for bringing me much needed sources to untangle the Gordian knot of Pantiya lineages, and for embarking on an Andal-Srivilliputtur project with me.

My intellectual *parampara* is not quite as neat as the Srivaisnava lineal descent from Nammalvar to Ramanuja. The gifts of knowledge I have accrued over the years from teachers, colleagues and friends are far-ranging and cross continents.

In the United States, Frank Clooney's painstaking work on Nammalvar and the commentaries on the *Tiruvaymoli* have deepened my own relationship to both. Working with Frank on the translation of the *Tiruvaymoli* challenged my conceptions and approach to translation itself. The mark of those early conversations about the *Tiruvaymoli* is indelible on what eventually became *A Hundred Measures of Time*. Leslie Orr, my go-to person on all things related to south Indian inscriptions, clarified with her usual ease and thoroughness some of my long-standing questions about Araiyar Cevai and *Tiruvaymoli* recitation. Vasudha Narayanan's *Vernacular Veda* was one of the first books on the *alvars* that I read many moons ago as a curious Berkeley undergraduate. It has stayed with me all these years, and was instrumental in getting me to engage with Nammalvar seriously. Conversations with Martha Selby on the relationship of Cankam literature (and the *Ainkurunuru* in particular) and bhakti poetry helped refine my readings of the *Tiruviruttam* and *Tirukkovaiyar*. David Shulman has been a generous, inspiring and patient interlocutor. His own long relationship with the *Tiruviruttam* has proved invaluable in my own journey. I eagerly anticipated his thoughtful comments in the form of early-morning emails on specific verses, which invariably pushed me to rethink, reconsider and revise. All of this and his sage counsel towards syllabic economy have made this a much better work. Davesh Soneji inspires with his scholarship and his kindness. His friendship and support over many years is a treasured blessing.

In Oxford, I was nourished by a vibrant set of thinkers and artists: Jim Robinson who ushered in a beautiful Durga on an elephant at exactly the right moment, Peggy Morgan who took me under her wing and showed me a little-known literary Oxford, Gavin Flood for his thought-provoking work on mysticism and Jessica Frazier for her detailed typologies of mystical experience that have done much to enhance my readings of Nammalvar.

In India, the staff of the French Institute of Pondicherry (IFP) has supported my research since my graduate days. Narendran, librarian of the IFP library, always managed to find me obscure sources. M. Kannan of the Contemporary Tamil Department at the IFP has been a dear friend, intellectual comrade and demanding interlocutor over many years. His friendship is one I cherish.

The people, priests, Araiyars and Kavis at Alvar Tirunagari brought Nammalvar alive for me through their performances and stories. Araiyar Srinivasan and Nathamuni's beautiful rendition of the *Tiruvaymoli* during the Markali festival in 2007 enlivened the text. Krishnan Kavi and Anaviyar Srinivasan first introduced me to Kavi Pattu, and rendered them with full-throated vigour on numerous occasions. It is through them that I came to appreciate the *Tiruviruttam*'s life in performance.

Kamini Mahadevan heard me present a somewhat confused paper on the *Tiruviruttam* during the very early stages of this project. At that time, she saw something in my work that I couldn't yet perceive, and she offered Penguin Classics as a home for the still nascent *Tiruviruttam*. It's taken almost as long as a hundred measures of time, but her gentle encouragement and stalwart patience through my innumerable delays eventually brought this book to safe harbour. I am grateful to my able navigators at Penguin, who brought to the project much calm professionalism: R. Sivapriya, editor of Penguin Classics, ably guided the work through its many stages; Olivia Fraser granted permission to use her painting *Radha* (2011) for the cover; Gavin Morris designed an arresting cover that does justice both to the painting and to the *Tiruviruttam*'s enigmatic contents; Richa Burman read the manuscript with sensitivity and thoroughness, treating the book as one of her own; Aparajita Ninan breathed new life into the faded lines of the images that accompany this book, and recreated for *A Hundred Measures of Time* the feel of books of a different era; and

Rimli Borooah with her keen vision curtailed grammatical crimes of various sorts.

My parents, Jayashree and Krishna Venkatesan, are my twin guiding lights. Their selfless love and abounding wisdom have given me a fearlessness to explore and push my boundaries. Even at my lowest moments, when this book seemed so far away, they never lost faith. I owe them everything. My sister, Aarathi, is a superwoman, an extraordinary example of courage and resolve. Her infectious laughter and unflagging belief in me have lighted my path and lightened my load on many a dreary day. Layne, my Red Earth, my Bright Star, I thank every day for you.

I have been blessed with gifted teachers and scholars who have shared themselves and their knowledge freely. They have taught me with sternness, with passion and compassion, with infinite attention and capacious understanding.

George Hart who first introduced me to Tamil poetry at Berkeley, when I didn't even know that such a thing as Cankam literature existed. I still recall the first day of my first class with him, when the thick description of an *Akananuru* poem soaked the air of a small room in Dwinelle. It was that moment that made me want to learn Tamil.

Sri Varadadesikar of the École française d'Extrême-Orient who brought warmth, joy and abiding *anubhava* to his expositions of Nammalvar. To witness his deeply felt anubhavas of the *Divya Prabandham* has been a privilege beyond measure. Through all this, he impressed on me, without ever meaning to, how to appreciate commentary for itself and not for what it could teach me about Nammalvar.

Steven Hopkins whose gentle goodness makes me aspire to be more than a good scholar. With a patient eye and unshakeable faith, through all the ups and downs, he has been teacher, mentor and friend. Whether we talk Blake or Keats, Andal or Desika, in poetry or prose, I always come away with more to think on, and moved beyond words.

Indira Viswanathan Peterson—how can I possibly articulate the enormous influence she has had on me? Her staggering, breathtaking command of south Indian literary history and culture has consistently pushed me towards interdisciplinarity. But it is her unstinting, unreserved intellectual giving that has inspired me to turn to her repeatedly for comfort and encouragement.

It is to these wonderful, gifted and generous intellectual giants that I dedicate this book, a humble short-knotted string of words.

A NOTE ON TRANSLITERATION

I have transliterated Tamil words according to the conventions of the *Tamil Lexicon*. Sanskrit-derived Tamil words are generally in their most easily recognizable form—so, Mādhavaṉ instead of Mātavaṉ. Place names that occur in the poems or in the commentary have been transliterated. In all other instances, place names adhere to their most common spelling. Names of contemporary authors and informants are rendered as they choose to spell them in English. I have transliterated the names of all historical personalities.

Tamil has twelve vowels, which are classified into five short vowels (*a*, *i*, *u*, *e*, *o*), five long vowels (*ā*, *ī*, *ū*, *ē*, *ō*), and two diphthongs (*ai* and *au*). There are eighteen consonants.

Below is a pronunciation guide.

Vowels

a pronounced like the *u* in *cut*

ā pronounced like the *a* in *father*

i	pronounced like the *i* in ***it***
ī	pronounced like the *ee* in ***feet***
u	pronounced like the *u* in ***put***
ū	pronounced like the *oo* in ***root***
e	pronounced like the *e* in ***set***
ē	pronounced like the *a* in ***rate***
o	pronounced like the *uo* in ***quo**te*
ō	pronounced like the *o* in ***go***
ai	pronounced like the *ie* in ***pie***
au	pronounced like the *ow* in ***cow***

Consonants

k (guttural)	pronounced like the *k* in ***k**ite*. Tamil e.g. ***k**al* (stone)
c (palatal)	pronounced like the *ch* in ***ch**alk*. It can also be pronounced as a sibilant, like the *s* in *sieve*. Tamil e.g. ***c**ol* (word)
ṭ (retroflex)	pronounced like the *t* in ***t**oe*. Tamil e.g. *vaṇṭu* (insect)
t (dental)	pronounced like the *t* in ***th**ing*. Tamil e.g. *vantu* (having come)
p	pronounced like the *p* in ***p**ro**p***. Tamil e.g. ***p**āl* (milk)
ṅ (nasal paired with *k*)	pronounced like the *nk* in *li**nk***. Tamil e.g. *maṅkai* (girl)
ñ (nasal paired with *c*)	pronounced like the *gn* in ***gn**osis*. Tamil e.g. *neñcu* (heart)
ṇ (nasal paired with *ṭ*)	pronounced like the *n* in *frie**n**d*. Tamil e.g. *vaṇṭu* (insect)
n (nasal paired with *t*)	pronounced like the *n* in ***n**ow*. Tamil e.g. *va**n**tu* (having come)

ṉ (alveolar nasal, occurs at the end of Tamil words)	Also pronounced like the *n* in ***now***, but with tongue pressed closer to the tongue. Tamil e.g. *ava**ṉ*** (he)
m (nasal paired with *p*)	pronounced like the *m* in ***m**arriage*. Tamil e.g. ***m**ayil* (peacock)
y	pronounced like the *y* in ***y**our*. Tamil e.g. ***y**ār* (who)
r	pronounced like the *r* in *you**r***. Tamil e.g. *yā**r*** (who)
ṟ	pronounced like the *dr* in ***dr**ill*. Tamil e.g. *a**ṉṟ**u* (then)
l	pronounced like the *l* in ***l**ight*. Tamil e.g. *i**l**ai* (leaf)
ḷ (retroflex)	pronounced like the *l* in ***bl**ah*, but with more emphasis. It is pronounced with the tongue curled back, akin to a kind of gargling sound. Tamil e.g. *ava**ḷ*** (she)
v	pronounced like the *v* in ***v**ictory*. Tamil e.g. ***v**il* (bow)
ḻ	No English equivalent. Pronounced as a gentle rolled sound similar to the North American use of the *r* sound as *American*. Tamil e.g. *e**ḻ**il* (beauty)

PRAVEŚAM

Entering the World of the *Tiruviruttam*

The *Tiruviruttam* is a compact, hundred-verse poem composed by the remarkable Tamil Vaiṣṇava mystic and poet, Śaṭhakōpaṉ-Nammāḻvār (c. eighth–ninth century CE).[1] Rendered in a series of interlinked verses, the poem maps and traverses a complex emotional terrain. It is framed as a love story that unfolds between an anonymous heroine (*talaivi*) and her beloved hero (*talaivaṉ*), while friends, fortune tellers, bees, birds and the poet's own heart play important supporting roles, acting as messengers, lamenters and audiences in a story everyone knows well. These stock characters are what A.K. Ramanujan referred to in his translation of Nammāḻvār as 'returning voices', pointing out the contiguity of antecedent Tamil Caṅkam poetics and Tamil bhakti poetry.[2] Traditional Śrīvaiṣṇava exegesis too recognizes this debt, identifying the *Tiruviruttam*'s frame as the *anyāpadeśārtha* or 'other' meaning. From this vantage, the *anyāpadeśa* is the poem's outer shell, serviceable and necessary, protecting the ripe, mature fruit of esoteric import (*svāpadeśārtha*) which it encases. Thus the poem can be read either as a beautiful and moving love story, which according to generations of Śrīvaiṣṇava scholars is to miss the point entirely, or as speaking certain fundamental and essential truths about the most pressing existential questions: the nature of life, of birth, of god, of one's own self. The poet himself oscillates between these two poles: the heroine's plaintive voice expressing the corporeal and emotive textures of her love for Viṣṇu, while a direct contemplative address reflects on Viṣṇu's unimaginable, inexpressible grandeur.

The *Tiruviruttam* is a quintessential Tamil bhakti poem. The object of love, of desire, of dedication, is god, identified by the poet as Viṣṇu-Nārāyaṇa. The expression of that love is corporeal, emotional and ecstatic, its expression poetic, abstract and symbolic. Viṣṇu is the divine, omnipresent sovereign and also the intimate, often absent, beloved. The relationship between the poem's chief participants is one of dependence, like a bard who relies on a generous king's largesse, and a woman who trusts in the inviolable love of her beloved. The divine king is the poet's sole refuge and the largesse sought is grace. *Tiruviruttam* 85 is an apt illustration of the ideology of dependence and subservience that gives Tamil bhakti poetry so much of its emotive force:

> Like a monkey tossing aside a ruby
> evening falls
> casting aside the golden sun
>
> O precious gem who measured worlds
> my beloved emerald
> golden one who has no equal
> you're the sole refuge of your servant's life.

Here Viṣṇu is the world-strider, an illustration of his awesome and indisputable supremacy, and the poet assumes a suitably abject position when approaching this supreme deity as the exclusive source and site of refuge. Yet it is the unique intimacy that they share which emboldens Nammāḻvār to dare such a bold petition. Viṣṇu is his, possessed by him and possessing him. He is *his* gem, *his* glittering ruby and, in other verses, *his* honey, *his* sweetness, *his* beloved.

Even as the *Tiruviruttam* is representative of the genre of Tamil bhakti poetry, it can be seen as both heir and progenitor in a long and illustrious lineage of Tamil poetry. The poem's frame, its succinct phrasing, its evocative and striking imagery and the seamless integration of the aesthetic principles of the public (*puṟam*) and private (*akam*) Caṅkam genres reveal its debt to what we know today as the Tamil classical literary traditions. The manipulation of these very principles to craft a narrative of love and loss, of separation and union, places the *Tiruviruttam* at the forefront of literary innovations that give us later medieval Tamil genres such as the *kōvai*, the *ulā* and, as David Shulman suggests, the *kalampakam*. I discuss these streams of influence in depth in Part II (The Measure of Time) of this book, and therefore refrain from repeating them here. Below, I offer a brief overview of *āḻvār* poetry and Nammāḻvār's place within it.

The Poetry of the Āḻvārs

A.K. Ramanujan titled his landmark translation of selected Nammāḻvār verses *Hymns for the Drowning*. It is an allusion to the title 'āḻvār', 'those who are immersed', granted to the twelve pioneering saints of the Śrīvaiṣṇava *saṁpradāya*s (lineages). The epithet expresses the fluid, emotional and immersive experience that characterizes the poetry of the Tamil Vaiṣṇava tradition. Yet, like Ramanujan's title, it also plays on the metaphor of the world as an ocean of sorrow in which Viṣṇu and his heavenly Vaikuṇṭha are the sole life-rafts. Āṇṭāḷ, a later contemporary of Nammāḻvār, says this in *Nācciyār Tirumoḻi* 5.4:

My bones melt and my eyes
long as spears
resist even blinking.
for days now, I am plunged into a sea of distress
and I ache to attain
that great boat, Vaikuṇṭha,
but I cannot see it.

O *kuyil*, you too know
the anguish of separation
from a beloved.
Summon the immaculate lord
    whose body is like gold
    whose banner bears Garuḍa
to me[3]

Āṇṭāḷ's verse evocatively captures the existential crisis at the centre of āḻvār poetry. As ecstatics, their experience of Viṣṇu is totalizing and complete, but as human beings the caprices of human birth are inescapable. This crisis expresses itself in their poetry as a dialectic of union and separation; the poet invariably speaks from a position of loss and absence, yet remains with eyes unblinking (see, for instance, *Tiruviruttam* 97 and 98) ever alert for a vision of the divine beloved.

The *Paripāṭal*, an abstract and fragmentary Tamil anthology from the late fourth century CE (?), may be regarded as containing the earliest record of praise and devotion to Māl (Viṣṇu), leading Kamil Zvelebil to claim that it is 'probably the earliest literary testimony of the *bhakti* movement in South India, if not in India as a whole'.[4] The *Paripāṭal*, composed in the metre of the same name, originally consisted of seventy poems, but only twenty-two are extant, many of which are fragments. Of these twenty-two, six are dedicated to Tirumāl (the Tamil name for Viṣṇu), eight to Cevvēl (Murukaṉ) and eight to the river Vaikai. Demonstrating the influence of Caṅkam literary conventions and practices, the radically new poems of the *Paripāṭal* anthology appropriate the themes of love (the private, that is, akam) and heroism (the public, that is, puṟam) to express the new sensibility of devotion. While love (akam) dominates the mood of the Vaikai poems, the elements of war and heroism (puṟam) colour those dedicated to the great warrior deities, Cevvēl and Māl. In the *Paripāṭal* poems, the panegyric, a staple of puṟam poetry, becomes the favoured mode to produce poetry that is 'simultaneously devotional and heroic'.[5] These early expressions (and literary experiments) of devotionalism often express themselves in oblique, speculative language, a register that is at first glance rather different from the passionate compositions of the later Tamil bhakti poets. But just as the *Paripāṭal* bears the marks of its literary past, the *mutal āḻvār*—Poykai, Pēy, Pūtam—who probably lived in the late seventh century, demonstrate an unmistakable continuity with the speculative tone and luminous mode of the *Paripāṭal*. There is high philosophy and even higher praise, all ensconced in deeply felt sentiment, an intricate embroidery of words that creates the very body of god to generate texts for visualization and poems of vision.

The early āḻvārs—Poykai, Pēy, Pūtam and Tirumaḻicai—usher in a sustained period of poetic innovation and philosophical syncretism over approximately two centuries. Although the Śrīvaiṣṇava tradition chooses to remember and revere twelve poets as their pioneering founders, there certainly must have been other contemporary poets and philosophers of a similar persuasion. Indeed, the famous narrative of recovery of the four thousand songs of the āḻvārs reflects a reality in which texts, both oral and written, were often lost to the indiscriminate pressures of memory and nature.[6] Further, the twelve poets with their distinctive voices and equally distinctive backgrounds signal an emergent sect's desire to encompass the whole of society. Thus, we can count among the āḻvārs robbers, kings, peasants, a woman, a lowly musician and many Brahmins. They embrace a range of poetic possibilities: the passionate love-longing of the woman Āṇṭāḷ, the crooning lullabies of Periyāḻvār and Kulaśekaran̲, the abstract philosophical articulations of Nammāḻvār, his disciple Maturakavi's moving tribute to his teacher, the 'untouchable' musician Tiruppaṇāḻvār's exultant, dense descriptions of god's body, Tirumaṅkai's virtuosic command of a variety of genres. The twelve āḻvārs together represent the coalescence of many voices around the central themes of loving service, ecstatic love, a tightly bound devotional community—all in the celebration of Viṣṇu's presence in this world, his immanence and his transcendence—and of the mutual dependence between god and devotee.[7]

Vaiṣṇava Tamil bhakti poetry is forged in the confluence of multiple streams. Caṅkam poetry provides the aesthetic vocabulary and emotional depth, the Sanskrit epics, Purāṇas and local mythology add texture and grandeur, and the edifice of the Pāñcarātra tradition imbue the poems with esotericism. A.K. Ramanujan and Norman Cutler were right to assert in their seminal essay on the transformation of classical Tamil poetics into the new literary genre of bhakti poetry, that the poets 'used whatever they had at hand, and changed whatever they used'.[8]

Although bhakti poetry has often been characterized as revolutionary in spirit, its egalitarian ethos did not translate into a rejection of Sanskrit scriptural sources. Indeed, the poets' use of these sources (scriptural or mythological) reveals a complex engagement with the Sanskrit traditions, one that belies simple formulae of rejection or appropriation. Āḻvār poetry often evokes the authority of the Vedas, lauding those who master the Vedas, while also arguing the converse, that knowledge of the Vedas is no guarantee for a vision of god. Nammāḻvār's poetry offers a typically nuanced articulation of these very ideas (*Tiruviruttam* 44):

She Said:

The texts of philosophy may speak
of his colour his ornaments his beauty
his names his forms . . .

although they hold aloft
the bright light of lofty knowledge everywhere
they still cannot see
the greatness of my lord.

Viṣṇu is praised as the [source of] Vedas (*Tiruviruttam* 79) and the presence of epithets like Taittiriyan (he who is the *Taittirīya Upaniṣad*) and Vētaṉ (he who is the Veda) serve to capture the indivisible relationship between Viṣṇu and the Vedas, the foundational texts of Brahminical ritual praxis.[9] Though the impulse of bhakti was radical in a number of ways—advocating community, enfolding women and lower castes as part of the group, asserting the efficacy of devotion as an equalizer before god—it also stressed the value of Sanskritic, Brahminical temple-based ritual and liturgical traditions. Thus, while women and lower-caste groups are counted among the twelve āḻvār—Nammāḻvār himself belonged to a landowning lower-caste group (Vēḻḻāla), it was not simply a movement '*by* the lowly, *for* the lowly',[10] and the choice to compose in Tamil rather than Sanskrit was not a revolutionary act of rebellion but, as the poems of the *Paripāṭal* demonstrate, one that emerged organically from the rich Tamil literary past.

It should come as no surprise then that the āḻvārs fiercely assert the value of the Tamil tradition, claiming for their works an elevated literary status. The poems' *phala śrutis* (closing verses) guarantee the reciter a good life in Vaikuṇṭha or excellent progeny not only because they praise Viṣṇu, but because they do so in the highest, sweetest Tamil. While Nammāḻvār doesn't make the claim in the *Tiruviruttam*, it is oft-repeated in the concluding verses of the *Tiruvāymoḻi*. For example:

> Those mastering this ten from the melodious Tamil thousand
> about the dark-bodied lord with large red eyes
> by the one who lives in rich Valuti with its groves filled with bees
> will rule heaven and achieve the great release.
>
> *Tiruvāymoḻi* II.8.11[11]

In other words, the Tamil literary tradition and local mythologies were just as alive as those of the Sanskrit world. The āḻvār poems are littered with allusions to myths that cannot be traced to Sanskrit sources, and instead reflect the circulation and integration of a local Vaiṣṇava mythology.[12]

The most important elements of āḻvār devotion such as singing god's praise, performing acts of loving service to him and his devotees, singing the greatness of his sacred abodes resonate with the key elements of heroic puṟam poetry that highlighted the intimate, symbiotic relationship between a king and his bard. In bhakti poetry, the fierce, generous Tamil king becomes the omnipresent deity and the devotee is his willing supplicant and poet.[13] Viṣṇu is the patron who protects the poet not just from the prosaic concerns of daily living, but from the very bonds of endless birth. If the puṟam elements of bhakti poetry express the transcendence of god, the rich treasure house of akam love poetry reveals the intimacy between god and devotee. The mingling of the complementary categories of akam and puṟam in Tamil Vaiṣṇava poetry reflect the twin, inseparable aspects of god's nature, his transcendence and immanence, his remoteness and his accessibility. *Tiruviruttam* 85 characterizes Viṣṇu as the one 'who measured the world' and as the peerless golden one, words worthy of a lofty divine sovereign. Yet he is also addressed with typical Tamil endearments as the poet's own 'precious gem' and his 'beloved emerald'.

Such layering of epic, Purāṇic and local mythology over the deft manipulation of poetic conventions shape ideas about the relationship between Viṣṇu and his devotees and is typical of bhakti poetry. The Rāmāyaṇa is a particularly useful source offering up numerous examples of a devotee's paradigmatic surrender, of god's boundless grace and of the fundamentally reciprocal relationship between god and his devotees. Poets like Periyāḻvār and Kulaśekara innovate within the established framework, imagining themselves often as god's doting parents or his caretakers, reversing the traditional relationship of dependence between Viṣṇu and his devotee. Indeed, Periyāḻvār earns the epithet 'Great Āḻvār' precisely because he sang the *Tiruppallāṇṭu*, his famous song of protection (*kāppu*) for Viṣṇu.

A still third element in the making of āḻvār poetry is that of the Pāñcarātra Āgamas. The origin and history of the

Pāñcarātra is somewhat obscure, and various explanations have been provided to unearth the significance of the five nights alluded to in the name Pāñcarātra (literally, Five Nights). It has been taken to refer to five dialogues, five kinds of knowledge (where the word *rātra*, night, is taken to mean *jñāna*, knowledge), the five forms of Viṣṇu or five kinds of sacrifice/worship. Most Vaiṣṇava saṁpradāyas follow the liturgy, ritual formulations and methodologies laid out in the corpus of approximately two hundred Pāñcarātra texts. Vasudha Narayanan has described the contribution of the Pāñcarātra Āgamas to the development of the Tamil Vaiṣṇava tradition as akin to the invisible, subterranean river Sarasvati at the confluence of the Ganga and Yamuna at Prayag.[14] Although the Pāñcarātra references are not explicit, the āḻvār emphasis on the worship of the icon in a temple and the mention of Viṣṇu's five forms indicate that the esotericism of these ritual manuals significantly shaped the direction of Vaiṣṇava bhakti in Tamil country.[15]

These early experiments marrying an emergent philosophy, ideology and poetic aesthetic matured into the works of the āḻvār poets over a period of two and a half centuries (c. 600–850 CE). Late poets like Nammāḻvār and Tirumaṅkai are masters of multiple genres and metres, authoring monumental poems that run into several thousand verses. Approximately a century after Tirumaṅkai (c. late eighth century), the compositions of the āḻvārs were collected into a compilation of four thousand poems known as the *Nālāyira Divya Prabandham* (The Divine Collection of Four Thousand). Around the same period, the emergent community of Tamil Vaiṣṇavas (who come to be known as the Śrīvaiṣṇavas) began to develop a sophisticated theology called Ubhaya Vedānta (dual Vedānta). Within this system, the Tamil poems of the a̲lvār poets were placed on par with the Sanskrit Veda and both sets of texts were considered revealed. Thus, the Śrīvaiṣṇava traditions refer to the *Nālāyira Divya Prabandham* as the Tamil̲ Veda or the Drāviḍa Veda. Even while the entire *Nālāyira Divya Prabandham* is considered revealed, one poet and one poem are marked as particularly special. Nammāl̲vār, who refers to himself by the name Śaṭhakōpan̲ or Mār̲an̲, is the most significant of the twelve poets, and his four compositions—*Tiruviruttam*, *Tirvāciriyam*, *Periya Tiruvantāti* and *Tiruvāymol̲i*—are considered equivalent to the Vedic Saṁhitā texts. Of these four works, the *Tiruviruttam* and *Tiruvāymol̲i* are given pride of place, with the former being associated with the *Ṛg Veda* and the latter with the *Sāma Veda*.[16]

The Śrīvaiṣṇava commentarial traditions regard claims about the revelatory character of the *Tiruviruttam* and the *Tiruvāymol̲i* as emerging from the texts themselves. Revelation in the *Tiruviruttam* manifests in verses that deliberately break the love-story frame. The story of the anonymous lovers is inexplicably set aside for a verse in which the poet presumably speaks in his own voice, or, as he asserts, in god's words. Below is one of the first such instances:

Little worms that live in a wound
do what they do.
What do they know of the world?

I learned these songs from that cunning Tirumāl
who uses me to sing of himself.
It's like people making meaning
from the chirp of a lizard.

Tiruviruttam 48

Medieval commentaries on this verse (c. thirteenth century) interpret it as a confirmation of revelation, that Nammāḻvār's compositions are not his own creation. He is simply the conduit through which Viṣṇu reveals himself. We can find several similar examples in the *Tiruvāymoḻi* as well. In the seventh book of the *Tiruvāymoḻi* (VII.9.1), the poet makes the following claim:

> What can I say of the Lord
> who lifted me up for all time,
> and made me himself, every day?
> My radiant one, the first one,
> My Lord, sings of himself,
> through me, in sweet Tamil.[17]

Here the speaker of the poem, identified with Nammāḻvār, sees himself not as the instrument through which Viṣṇu acts; rather, he is the means through which god reveals himself by singing his own praise. Nammāḻvār's articulation of revelation in both the *Tiruviruttam* and *Tiruvāymoḻi* is couched in the language of possession. The poet has simply given himself over to Viṣṇu, becoming a capacious vessel, the translucent medium through which god acts, speaks and reveals himself. Yet, such possession also expresses the fundamental intimacy and mutual dependency between god and devotee, a relationship upon which Vaiṣṇava bhakti poetry is predicated. Even as Nammāḻvār disavows a hand in his own work, his disciple Maturakavi makes a startling claim in his short panegyric *Kaṇṇi Nuṉ Ciṟu Tāmpu*. Here, it is Nammāḻvār who is the source of grace (verse 3), who possesses the student, who teaches him the truth of the Vedas (verses 6, 9). Moments like those cited above from the *Tiruviruttam* and the *Tiruvāymoḻi* alongside Maturakavi's dramatic claims about the revelatory character of his teacher's works become the foundation upon which the Śrīvaiṣṇavas develop the theory of Ubhaya Vedānta, ultimately claiming for these compositions (and the entire *Nālāyira Divya Prabandham*) the title of Drāviḍa Veda/Tamiḻ Veda.

About the Translation

The project to translate the *Tiruviruttam* began in 2007. In that year, I read the poem alongside the medieval commentaries of Periyavāccāṉ Piḷḷai and the modern ones authored by Uttamur Veeraraghava Acarya, Annakaracharya and Satakopan Ramanujacarya, making my way slowly, one verse at a time, trying to make sense of its complexity, both literary and theological. Although I had read the poem several times before, this was the first time I read it through the lens of commentary. The tradition's own interpretation of the poem's multiple layers informed my impressions and ultimately determined the very form of this book.

My translation strives for fidelity, a fidelity to the words of the text and its emotion, and owes much to the Śrīvaiṣṇava intellectual traditions in which it has been nurtured over many centuries. Since I discuss the nitty-gritty details of translation in the accompanying essay 'The Measure of Time', I will not reproduce them here. In its place I offer a brief overview of method, of how the English translation came to inhabit its current shape. I take as an example *Tiruviruttam* 76, identified as spoken in the voice of the heroine, and share several early drafts to demonstrate my translation process, and the choices that led to the current version. It is almost customary to paraphrase Valery's famous quote: a translation is never finished, only abandoned, and below I chart the path that brought me to abandonment.

iṭam pōy virintu iv ulaku aḷantāṉ eḻil ār taṇ tuḻāy
Vaṭam pōtil naiyum maṭa neñcamē naṅkaḷ veḷ vaḷāikkē
Viṭam pōl virital itu viyappē viyaṉ tāmaraiyiṉ
Taṭam pōtu oṭuṅka mel āmpal alarvikkum veṇ tiṅkaḷē

Tiruviruttam 76 in Tamil

In a very early 'zero-draft' I laid out *Tiruviruttam* 76 on facing pages of a long notebook. On the right side of the ruled notebook I carefully wrote out the Tamil in bright blue ink, with all the *sandhi* (morphophonemic rules) in place. Below it, in pencil, the Tamil again with the sandhi broken and notated with odd squiggles and brackets indicating words, phrases, and so on, which are linked grammatically and thematically. Further down, also in pencil, rough English equivalents, staccato-like, nouns, verbs, adverbs and participles following each other, connected with more esoteric squiggles and brackets. The first translation, composed almost in prose, bare of punctuation and sans diacritical marks, runs below the Tamil text and endeavours to follow word and line order and strives to replicate Tamil grammatical forms in English as far as possible:

> he measured this world, having come down and expanding (*virintu*)—his lovely, cool, special tulasi garland's buds that [is] desired by innocent/naive heart [The innocent heart that desires his lovely, cool, special tulasi of him who measured . . .]
>
> [for] my white bangles it spreads like poison—is this surprising! [Is it a surprise/what a surprise!]—the bright white moon that closes the broad/large buds of the awesome/excellent lotus and blossoms the delicate *ambal*.

Even in this very early draft I had already made translation choices that would carry through the many revisions. The Tamil *tul̲āy* (sacred basil, *Ocimum tenuiflorum*) was rendered into the Sanskrit *tulasī* almost instinctively, and the Tamil *āmpal* (*Nymphaea lotus*), an indigenous water lily, remained as such, making this English translation not wholly English at all.

Below the prose version appeared brief notes about the verse, written in ink, based on my reading of Periyavāccān̲ Pil̤l̤ai. These were meant to act as my guide to both understanding the verse and its interpretation. The italicized, transliterated words in the text below indicate those that were written out in Tamil script in my notebook.

> This verse is spoken by the talaivi after a separation follows the union indicated in the previous verse. The despairing heroine addresses her own heart, calling it innocent/naive (maṭa neñcam) for it desires the garland of tulasi, something that is difficult to obtain. Even things that were at one point friends have become enemies, like the moon. She accuses it of being stupid and indiscriminate, unable to differentiate between exalted and lowly things. The verse may either be taken as the heroine speaking to her friend, or speaking/offering consolation to her own heart.
>
> In this verse she desires the garland that he wore during the Trivikrama Avatāra, for this garland demonstrates that he is the master of the whole world. Moreover, it is made beautiful because it touches his skin/body (tirumēn̲i). Thus her heart is described as maṭa neñcam as it desires an unattainable object and despairs when it does not realize that desire.

> The moonlight spreads like a poison and appears to the talaivi that the moon desires her bangles because she says that he (the moon) thinks that he has a right to it being in form and color like him (white).

Guided by the commentaries' emphasis on the heroine's hopeless, naive heart, I began the English translation with the phrase *maṭa neñcam* (innocent heart), although the Tamil text begins with a grand description of Viṣṇu spreading everywhere. This choice was made easier still because the heart (*neñcam*) is also the subject of the long sentence that makes up the first two lines of the Tamil text, all that precedes *neñcam* serving to qualify it: the [this] innocent heart that desires the tulasī of the one who measured the world. But I did not want the translation to make explicit the connections Piḷḷai draws out. So in its first transfiguration from prose to poetry, *Tiruviruttam* 76 became this, written in English (again, with little punctuation and no diacritics) on the facing page:

> My innocent heart desires
> the buds in the garland of lovely, cool tulasi
> (that adorns) the one who measured the world.
> [rising and growing and spreading everywhere]
> So is it surprising that this white moonlight
> spreads like poison everywhere, wanting my white bangles—
> this silly moon which causes the excellent lotus to close
> its broad petals and the lovely ambal to bloom.

The initial verse version was concerned with determining how the lines might look on the page. How did I want the images to follow and succeed? What sequence of sounds did I want to replicate? By this point in my translation, almost three-quarters of the way through, I had set myself an impossible goal of trying to translate Nammāḻvār's densely packed four-line verses into equally dense eight lines of English blank verse. Some verses from the *Tiruviruttam* lent themselves to this format almost without effort, but others, especially those with a string of embedded clauses and cascading adjectival participles defied the discipline I sought to impose both on myself and on the poem. Nonetheless, I persisted, translating all hundred four-line verses of the *Tiruviruttam* into their eight-line English-language counterparts.

Eventually, several drafts and experiments later, the verse began to find a form that I felt reflected the dual structure of the verses and the poem's two levels of meanings. It identified the speaker of the poem, following a practice (What She Said/ She Said) that has become a convention among translators of Tamil Caṅkam poetry. While I debated the value of this intrusion primarily because the text makes no such identification, I eventually decided in favour of its inclusion, partly as a nod to the commentaries, which do. Not only do these identifications bring out the dramatic and dialogic quality of the *Tiruviruttam*, they also enable those verses that break the frame or are composed in a purely metaphysical mode to stand out in stark contrast. So version ten/twenty/ fifty-five, draped in diacritics and showy italics, and preserved in an ephemeral electronic form, looked something like this:

She Said:

My innocent heart desires
the buds of cool, lovely *tulasī* that adorn
the one who spread everywhere
and measured this world

Is it any surprise that the white moon
    that closes the broad petals of the lovely lotus
    and makes the delicate *āmpal* bloom
should spread like poison everywhere
wanting my white bangles?

As I began to play with a leaner and more succinct translation register, one that I felt was closer to Nammāḻvār's compact and economical style, the translated lines became shorter, the punctuation was reduced to a bare minimum, and eventually, the intrusive italicization of Indic words was discarded:

She Said:

My innocent heart desires
the buds of cool lovely tulasī that adorn
the one who spread everywhere
measured this world

Is it a surprise the white moon
    closes the broad petals of the lovely lotus
    makes the delicate āmpal bloom
spreads like poison everywhere
wanting my white bangles?

And finally, to reproduce the experience (*anubhava*) of reading the *Tiruviruttam* in Tamil from one of those early printed editions of Śrīvaiṣṇava books, which intersperse text with enchanting line drawings of Viṣṇu, his consorts, his symbols and the āḻvārs, some of those very images have been inserted into the pages of *A Hundred Measures of Time*.* The images have been sourced from three books in a collection of approximately 400 old Śrīvaiṣṇava books gifted to me by Prof. George Hart. Prof. Hart acquired them several decades ago from Prof. K.K.A. Venkatachari, who brought the libraries of two old Teṅkalai scholars to the United States. This impressive collection represents some of the earliest publications of Śrīvaiṣṇava scholarship, most of which was centred in the colonial port city of Madras.

Bringing the *Tiruviruttam* into English has not just been about finding proper linguistic equivalents and an equally proper emotional tenor. It has lived and been nurtured by generations of Śrīvaiṣṇava scholars, who have found ever new things to read and see in this magnificent poem. It is indeed a literary work of startling power and depth, but lest we forget, it is above all a religious poem, one that lays out Nammāḻvār's compelling personal vision of god's nature and of his relationship to that divine being, whom he identifies as Viṣṇu-Nārāyaṇa.

* The images used here are from—p. xx: 'Nammāḻvār' from *Tiruviruttam* (Cennapaṭṭaṇamu: Śrīnikētana Mudrākṣaraśālā, c. 1903–04); p. 22: 'Viṣṇu avatāra Varāha' and p. 76: 'Viṣṇu' both from *Śrī Vēṅkaṭācala Māhātmya Graṃtha* by Śrīrāmakiśōradāsajī Nāmadhēyasya (Cennapurī: Kalāratnākara Mudrākṣaraśālā, c. 1896); and p. 178: 'Nammāḻvār' from *Tiruvāymoḻi* (Cennapaṭṭaṇamu: Śrīnikētana Mudrākṣaraśālā, c. 1903–04). My thanks to Davesh Soneji for his aid in transliterating the Telugu script on the copyright pages of these books.

PART I

A HUNDRED MEASURES OF TIME

Nammāḻvār's *Tiruviruttam*

1

False wisdom wicked conduct dirty bodies
let's not draw near such things now

To protect life
you took birth from many wombs

O master of the unblinking ones

stand before me embodied
listen graciously to a servant's plea.

2

Her Friend Said:

Her eyes with their fine red lines
    dart like kayal in a full pond
O let her live
that woman with dense curly hair

her love adorns the feet
of Kaṇṇa<u>n</u> dark as heavy rain clouds
worshipped by the ancient ones
who live in the sky.

3

She Said:

Seeing
    the gentle woman dear to the flute-playing cowherd
Seeing
    goddess earth and Śrī
    inseparable as his shadow
will it remain there or return to me:

my lonely heart followed the bird
    of the king whose fiery disc
    scorches like his cool lovely tulasī
that bird praised by the gods
that bird whose anger burns like fire.

4

She Said:

His bird already stole my lonely heart
now I have no heart left
for his cool beautiful tulasī
to steal.

O cool venomous māruta breeze
intruding here with tulasī
that adorns the hair of the one
who suckled the breast of the deceitful demoness
my life shivers:
Is this your nature?

5

Her Friend Said:

At this time in this city
the cool breeze abandons its nature
forgets everything breathes fire.
Is it to ruin the lustre of the girl
whose broad eyes spill tears like rain?

She weeps for cool lovely tulasī
from the one dark as rain clouds
whose sceptre has bowed
this one time.

6

He Said:

Who is this girl
eyes broad as arrows
brows curved like bows
whose shy glance retreats from improper things
a gently swaying creeper?

She is death
mastered by the sceptre of the one
who destroys demons
who rides that swift bird
whose son is sweet Madana
Shelter your life in this world.

7

Her Friend Said:

Those are two dark strong bulls in the sky
drenching the world in their sweat
as they paw the ground and fight
or is it
the cool season in Tirumāl's form
come to mock the suffering of those left behind?

I don't know which it is
bound by terrible fate, I see this.

8

She Said:

If we consider all he does
listen to all he says
we will realize
the lord of the mountain deceives.

He who lifted the tall mountain
has left for Vēṅkaṭam's cool tall hills
praised by the gods
to amass wealth:
his new resolve.

9

He Said:

O pretty creeper with flowers like gems
you are equal to the city in the sky
of the lovely lord who wields
an unyielding fiery disc
Who would leave you?

Are these eyes? Or
a dark neytal nestled in a bright lotus,
white pearl-like buds spill from the bright kuvaḷai.
O innocent fawn
your lips tremble like a tender leaf.

10

He Said:

O girls who are like creepers
of Māyōn's Tiruvēṅkaṭam
you refuse to listen
when I speak of my disease.

Is it your lovely lips or your voices
crying 'Ayyō!' at the parrot
that destroy me?
I am ill-fated.
Tell me. It's so hard to know.

11

He Said:

I've seen something rare today:
you are like Kaṇṇaṉ's celestial city,
yet one crosses vast distances in search of wealth

Lustrous pearls enough to buy the world
skin like pale gold
these large darting keṇṭai broad as the palm of my hand
are what one treasures.

12

She Said:

My jewel-like lustre fades
a thick dense paleness spreads all over me
the night is an aeon
and everything else is like this

such is the special wealth
bestowed upon my heart
bonded to Kaṇṇaṉ's cool lovely tulasī
my lord who wields the sharp disc.

13

She Said:

The reign of the blazing sun who alone rules the sky ended.
Cool dark night spreads through the world.
Who can stop the cool breeze that comes bearing tulasī
to stoke a love that brings only misery?

Who will protect my bangles?
O this aeon ravages me!

14

He Said:

Are her two eyes
spears that cut through me
or lovely fish that illumine my life
and don't draw back?

Are they radiant arrows of divine Kāma?
Or are these enchanting eyes two kayal
    searching for the city of the lord
    whose form is a brilliant dark fire?

15

The Friend Said:

You stand there asking
'Are your eyes kayal?'
'Did an elephant come this way?'
You are a stranger. We don't know you.
What words are these?

We have been here many many days
guarding the groves of the lord of Vēṅkaṭam
    dark as rain clouds that have drunk the sea.
Do you know us?

16

She Said:

It becomes many many aeons
It becomes tiny tiny moments
When we are together
When he is away

O friend equal to Kaṇṇaṉ's celestial city
such is the nature of this wide dense night
with its many many tricks.
I become frail. May it prosper.

17

She Said:

Wide as vast pervasive night
and your great crashing waves
O sea, may you prosper.
Don't erase the tracks of my beloved's chariot
who left in dead of night.

Like an all-encompassing brilliant black sun
he reclines on his serpent
that lord a radiant black flame
rests on you, O sea.

18

Her Friend Said:

The clouds swallowed the sea, rose up
and the furious ocean pursued them
to recover what was left.
Is now that time when the sea swells
to swallow Kaṇṇan̲'s earth and sky?

Is it the season of storms?
Or lovely one
perhaps these are your tears
that rain like waterfalls to fill the sea.

19

The Mother Said:

In the season of rains
dark rain clouds stacked in the sky
call out in challenge
'Who can guard a woman's heart?'

The one who rides the bird
he doesn't grant her his cool lovely tulasī
he doesn't grant her a little grace
now the village gossips about my quiet daughter.

20

The Friend Said:

The great god causes this quiet girl's disease.
It's not the disease of the young god
who demands things to end it.

O Vēlaṉ, stop now.
Mother, listen to me
Repeat the names of the one who swallowed the
seven worlds
adorn her with his garland of lovely cool tulasī.

21

Celestials in the sky
offer you pure perfect garlands anoint you with cool water
worship you with beautiful incense

you vanish by a trick

to scoop up and eat butter
to dance between the two sharp horns
of the humped bull
for the lovely woman of the strong cowherd clan.

22

The Friend Said:

In your hand you hold a leafy branch
you have no bow with which to hunt
yet you inquire about an elephant
you shot

Sir in this wide world
of that thief who rides the bird
no one speaks such things.
Is it to answer your odd questions
that we are here in this vast grove?

23

He Said:

I was passing by this grove.
My fate is terrible.
O women, tell me if you guard
my heart or this grove?

O you with eyes the colour
of a beautiful lotus grove
O you who are equal to the gods
who live in Kaṇṇaṉ's celestial city!
Is this your nature?

24

The Mother Said:

The disease—its nature is deception—
makes her eyes broad as one's palm
seem like darting fish in a vast ocean.

Her heart is fixed on the honey-drenched tulasī
        of the one who lifted the mountain
        to guard his flock from the rain
        that one who rides the bird.
What will happen to her beautiful bangles now?

25

She Said:

If my beautiful bangles make Kaṇṇaṉ's sceptre
which rules earth and sky
bend

what will it not do—that tulasī
dear to the king of valiant gods,
king of the heavens,
our king?

26

He Said:

O girl like gold, you crossed this wasteland
that the lovely fierce sun spat out
when he swallowed the four lands
and sucked them dry.

Look! Just beyond Kaṇṇan̲'s Veḥkā
where even gods come to pray
lie lovely cool flower gardens rich with honey
that give comfort no matter one's state.

27

She Said:

'A noble king's grace makes even enemies friends'
people delight in this truth.

The northern breeze called out a challenge
breathed fire all the time
now it touches Kaṇṇan̲'s garland of lovely cool tulasī
and is cooled.

28

She Said:

The cool lovely tulasī steals my bangles
I lose my lustre
The northern breeze wanders about
caressing me.

Grant me grace O lord of Tiruvaraṅkam
where even birds with sharp beaks
don't torment snails in the bountiful river.
Has there been another to suffer like this?

29

She Said:

'You two be my messenger. I have no one else'
yet without reply you and your mate
fly about the world of the great lord
whose dark body seems to swallow lightning.

O geese born in a clan with no virtues
is it the nature of a woman's messenger
to be like this?

30

She Said:

O geese, O herons, flying above
I entreat you. Whoever arrives first
don't forget

if you see my heart with Kaṇṇa<u>n</u>
lord of Vaikuṇṭha
    Tell him about me
    Ask him why he hasn't returned
    Inquire if *this* is his nature.

31

She Said:

If I say 'take my message'
they don't answer.
If I say 'wander above me'
will they obey?

O clouds, you bring bright lightning
to the lovely peaks of Tiruvēṅkaṭam
that glow with the radiance of gold and jewels.

32

She Said:

O clouds, what means did you use
to acquire a form like Tirumāl's?
Tell me.

To protect life you wander the vast sky
your aching bodies bearing water
your painful vow
that earned grace.

33

The Mother Said:

You rule vast sky and earth
with your disc that bestows grace
Your sceptre destroys cruel fate
dark as night

Isn't this woman worthy of protection?
Is she outside your dominion?
O lord who reclines on the serpent
We don't understand.
Her beauty is destroyed.

34

The Friend Said:

'This circle destroys me,' she said
and kicked at it in anger
with her pretty feet.

She is resolved to wear your garland
of dense cool lovely tulasī
I don't know what to do for this girl
who is now mad.

35

She Said:

Having lost the sun
the west wails cradling the moon at her waist
like a child, its mouth wet with milk
Such is the evening.

Those who love the tulasī
of the lord who measured worlds
have no relief
from the caress of the cold northern breeze.

36

She Said:

Now the endless long aeon arrives
using his cool garland as excuse
masquerades as the embrace
of deep swirling night.

Yet he remains without compassion.
He doesn't say 'Her suffering is long and endless.'
O mothers, such is the cruelty of the lord
who razed Laṅka's tall mansions.

37

The Mother Said:

For many years I worshipped
Kaṇṇaṉ's glorious feet adorned with flowers.
I was blessed
with this tender fawn-like girl whose waist is slender.
I am ill-fated.

She's taken the wide forest path
where hunters with curved bows
cattle rustlers murderous bandits
and fleet-footed youth beat drums
like the gossip of village women.

38

She Said:

You abandoned the forest
entered the pond to stand
on one foot.

O blue water lilies
is it from such penance
that you now have the form of the one
        who danced with pots
        who measured earth and sky
        made them tremble
        great lord who dances?

39

She Said:

Gleaming like a large lake of lotuses
on a dark vast mountain—
        lord of this world bound by surging oceans
        lord of the sky lord of the virtuous
        that dark lord
        my lord

I see the beauty of his eyes everywhere.

40

She Said:

O mothers richly adorned,
the beautiful bull-like sun hides behind the mountain
dark night spreads everywhere
like a herd of elephants.

When will I adorn my curly hair
with the tulasī
from Bhū and Śrī's beloved
O mothers, when will he glance at me?

41

She Said:

I know this lowly breeze from experience.
This time the suffering it inflicts is new
I don't know its form its special mark.

At this time that lord who rides the bird
destroys demons
but doesn't grant me grace.
The cruel breeze stays in the public square
to heap blame upon me.

42

She Said:

They gleamed
like tender lotuses blooming in a pond
swaying gently in the breeze
on their tender stalks.

'Look, my feet measure beyond earth and sky' he said
and touched the sky
I have surrendered to my lord
who glanced at me with his large radiant eyes.

43

She Said:

His eyes are red lotuses
His hands are red lotuses
His feet are red lotuses
His body is like a big dark mountain

Can those with great intellect or
those who crossed the sky or the gods
or even those who live beyond them
apprehend the beautiful form
of my lord?

44

She Said:

The texts of philosophy may speak
of his colour his ornaments his beauty
his names his forms . . .

although they hold aloft
the bright light of lofty knowledge everywhere
they still cannot see
the greatness of my lord.

45

She Said:

That large boar fixed his large lotus eyes upon me
in this terrible time
can there be anyone as blessed as me?

Tell me and live long, innocent heart,
can this swirling life, old and deep,
touch me again?

46

She Said:

Some send their heart as a messenger
to do their bidding
thinking 'It's an innocent heart, it's *my* heart.'
They should abandon such notions.

My steadfast heart left to place a message
at the feet of the one
who ripped the broad chest of the golden one
but it abandoned me, wanders even now.

47

Her Mother Said:

The cool northern breeze wanders.
The moon breathes white-hot fire
other things act the same.

Her refuge is Kaṇṇa<u>n</u>'s Vaikuṇṭha
        her conch bangles grow loose.
She desires the cool lovely tulasī
        paleness spreads over her skin.
Now what will happen to my tender girl?

48

Little worms that live in a wound
do what they do.
What do they know of the world?

I learned these songs from that cunning Tirumāl
who uses me to sing of himself.
It's like people making meaning
from the chirp of a lizard.

49

She Said:

O girl with lustrous brow
O girl equal to the earth that he
Madhusūdaṉaṉ Dāmodaraṉ
great lord
whose tulasī garlands dark bees feed on
eats spits out protects

Listen:
I've encountered this swollen night before
but I've neither seen nor heard nor known
a night that spreads like this.

50

He Said:

O skilled charioteer, drive quickly
Take me to her of the lustrous brow
before her colour fades

Take me to the great mountain
where waterfalls crash on the foothills
like strings of pearls from the tall crown of
Vaikuṇṭha's master,
one sweet as nectar.

51

She Said:

The ocean churned by the elusive lord
with a mountain as rod snake as rope
relented its nectar did not demand its return

Yet with fragrant tulasī as companion
it comes to torment me
to claim as its hereditary wealth
these conch bangles I bought from fisherfolk.

52

Her Friend Said:

When that woman born from the lotus
her eyes cool as rain rose
from the white waves of the roaring dark sea
climbed on to his serpent bed

the maiden of the earth lamented loudly in the sky
her tears poured as rivers
flowing down her breasts, these mountains,
She cried 'Tirumāl is cruel.'

53

The Fortune Teller Said:

This girl whose breasts are covered by cloth
has the divine disease
inflicted by the virtue
of the master of the gods.

Bring a garland of divine cool lovely tulasī
or even its leaves its stalk its roots
or just earth on which it grows
place it on her.

54

She Said:

O you with tiny feet and fluttering wings
it's easy for you to reach the city in the sky
tell me before you leave:
What will you say when you arrive?

Unite me
with the flawless flower-like feet
of the one who stole butter was scolded
for many such things
The king of gods is my lord, O bees.

55

He Said:

O bees, come here. I've something to ask you
You wander about drunk on honey
from flowers in water in trees in earth.

In all the wide places you wander
are there honey-drenched flowers
equal to the fragrance of the hair
of her equal to Vaikuṇṭha
    that place of the lord
    who rolled in the dust as a pig?

56

She Said:

Beautiful friend don't be afraid
we survived because of the grace
of the lord who swallowed this wide world

a breeze cool as a rain cloud
came bearing the sweet fragrance of lovely tulasī
it caressed my senses my jewels
but no one else knows.

57

He Said:

Her earrings entrance the senses.
In her lotus-like face her dark eyes dart like keṇṭai
whose war is blocked by a gently curving creeper
such eyes: wide and sharp as spears.

No one can mock me. Those eyes
bewilder me
I am like the ocean with its crashing waves
giving up its nectar
when Kaṇṇaṉ churned it with his mountain.

58

She Said:

One stride covered the earth
the next filled the sky
casting everything in its shade

Kaṇṇaṉ
who roams this vast world
a fiery light of ripe wisdom
higher than all beings
a lotus blossoming in a swamp
what is he going to measure here?

59

Her Mother Said:

'My love for his lovely cool tulasī
is longer greater deeper
than the endless terrible lovely ocean-like night.
He is Madhusūdaṉaṉ, master of wide fertile lands
bound by the ocean.'

It's my terrible fate
that she with a smile bright as jasmine buds
her red lips and broad breasts
should say such things
and I should hear them.

60

Her Mother Said:

Her breasts are still tender
Her dense fragrant hair is still short
She's half dressed most of the time
She babbles like a child
        the oceans the earth are no price
        for her darting bright eyes

Is it right for such a girl
to repeat what she's simply learned:
'Tiruvēṅkaṭam is the mountain!'

61

She Said:

Is it possible to speak
of the master of the ancient gods
of the one worshipped by all the gods
of him who in two strides
        spanned the entire world
        and not a blade of grass was spared
of the one born among cowherds?

He is our lord.

62

Her Mother Said:

O despite our pleas
the pitch-black ocean boasts 'Victory!'
It has no compassion for this one girl

Nothing but your grace can guard her modesty
there is no other protection.
O lord dark as rain clouds
one who reclines on the serpent
O tell me is this right?

63

She Said:

Are these those same eyes
cool gentle lotus, red and radiant,
a glance that comforts immortals in the sky?

I adore the beautiful face
of Kaṇṇaṉ Tirumāl
who inhabits my thoughts abides in me
his servant in this very moment.

64

She Said:

The masters of the earth cleave
to the weighty words of the Ṛg Veda
to praise faultlessly
the feet that spanned the worlds

I depressed subdued by fate
simply recite sacred names I've learned
like one who can't eat ripe fruit
and makes do with raw ones.

65

He Said:

Her eyes soft and gentle as a young doe's
defeat all others
Her eyes dart to their edges
as if to whisper secrets in her ear

Her bright eyes that may or may not have seen
the feet of the lord
who swallowed spat out worlds
devour me.

66

He Said:

These eyes entrance even yogis
who immersed in thought
neither eat nor sleep.

She is equal to Vaikuṇṭha
of the great lord who is fire water ether sky earth.
My fate may be terrible
but her eyes flower-red are my life.

67

He Said:

They vanquished red flowers dark flowers
spears kayal so many other things
and now her eyes desire my life.

She is like a lushly feathered bird
that lives in Vēṅkaṭam
land of Govindaṉ Mādhavaṉ
who destroyed demons
that one who rides the great bird.

68

Her Friend Said:

O girl like Vaikuṇṭha
of the great lord
who spanned this world surrounded by
swirling oceans
the lovely koṉṟai begin to bud
awaiting your lover's return

they haven't yet bloomed
into dense garlands of gold
that hang from a thick canopy of leaves.

69

The Friend Said:

The dark bull-like night lost to the fiery red morning
now it has returned desiring victory:
this brief lowly evening

O girl whose tender breasts are bound in cloth
don't despair for your bangles
Won't the tall lord who sealed a pact
and measured worlds
give you grace?

70

She Said:

I desired the dense fragrant garland
of cool lovely tulasī adorning the crown
of our lord of the heavens
who holds the beautiful curved disc

my lustre turned to paleness
when it came swiftly
stretching into days months years aeons
and now it's here to torture me
the night now a thousand aeons.

71

She Said:

I didn't say 'He became the end of days and
swallowed the seven worlds.'
I saw a dark fruit
observed 'It's the colour of the sea.'

My mother then said 'What impertinence!'
'She speaks of the colour of the one who
swallowed worlds.'
Speak to her dear friend. My mother scolds me.

72

She Said:

The lovely young moon that tears
the unshrinking dense darkness
of this endless swirling night
tears me too. It strengthens

I am alone
my heart fixed on the garland of tulasī.
Is this any way to live
waiting for my lustre to return?

73

Her Mother Said:

Like a white cow in the sky
the white moon spills its bright white moonlight
to delight the world,
evening ripens.

Is it right that the one who protects the seven worlds
    lord who holds the fiery disc
    that glows like the sun
allows this lonely girl to suffer so?

74

Her Friend Said:

His long eyes closed, he slumbers
upon his bed resting
on rolling rising ocean waves
When he comes awake
he swallows worlds

A fresh gentle breeze wafts
having devoured the fragrance of tulasī
adorning the crown of that same one
who uprooted the great mountain
turned it on its head.

75

He Said:

O your bright faces slay me
with their arrow-sharp eyes that dart like keṇṭai
and brows that curve like fearsome bows

Are you from Vaikuṇṭha where his devotees abide
    that place where the lord reclines
    on the sea with its lovely waves
    that push rounded conch shells to shore?
Or are you from this earth?

76

She Said:

My innocent heart desires
the buds of cool lovely tulasī that adorn
the one who spread everywhere
measured this world.

Is it a surprise the white moon
    closes the broad petals of the lovely lotus
    makes the delicate āmpal bloom
spreads like poison everywhere
wanting my white bangles?

77

She Said:

The beautiful young moon wails
when the sun falls on the crimson battlefield.

The lowly evening arrives with the tulasī
    of the master of the gods
    who made Laṅka a terrible battlefield
as a companion
to steal my beauty to torment me.

78

She Said:

He vanquished evil Naraka
He cut down Bāṇa's strong shoulders
I am unfit to speak of his courage his greatness

My innocent heart frantic
for the garland of lovely tulasī that adorns
the lord whose radiant form is like a dark mountain
brings me such suffering.

79

She Said:

He is the Veda. Adorned with a bright white thread
praised by the gods as their master
the one without end who swallowed worlds
whose feet measured worlds
who reclines on the serpent on the ocean of milk
He gives us grace

those who worship that gentle one are greater
than those who live in the sky.

80

She Said:

The sun has died
his reign brief as of a noble mortal king.
O king who measured the earth
O king of countless names
my king who rules the sky

O king who abandoned me with such cunning
give me grace
night has come to torment me.

81

Her Friend Said:

When they don't consider changes in her
can we say that these are her mothers
or this one gave birth to her?

They don't adorn her hair with tulasī
nor take her to ancient Vēṅkaṭam
to gain some relief.
Her body falls apart her gentle soul burns.

82

She Said:

My lord's eyes are like two fiery red suns
rising above the mountains of Udayagiri.
I am like demons who cast themselves
into the red fire that burns.

Tell me is this a measure
of his caring protection of the world?

83

Her Mother Said:

In the courtyard she saw the nest of twigs in the palm tree
thought of the a<u>nr</u>il's delicate call for its mate
then madly repeated the names
of the lord dark as rain clouds.

I don't know how my beautiful girl can survive
her fragile life ebbs her body is listless
Will it only end with her death?

84

She Said:

Amidst a throng of lovely women
or surrounded by crowds of virtuous priests
in some festival or in places like that

I long to see you
holding in your hands golden disc and white conch
O one dark as kohl my precious gem
pearl of mine my glittering ruby.

85

She Said:

Like a monkey tossing aside a ruby
evening falls
casting aside the golden sun.

O precious gem who measured worlds
my beloved emerald
golden one who has no equal
you're the sole refuge of your servant's life.

86

She Said:

You rid Aran cursed
to eat from a stinking skull
carved from Ayan's head,
the lotus-born one, you are his refuge

You who hold aloft disc and conch as weapons
stole butter then cried
when the cowherd woman bound you with ropes.
My lord what's left to say in my lament?

87

The Mother Said:

In a heavy full-throated voice the anril laments
In a loud voice waves crash into beautiful
salt marshes
hearing this
she praised the virtues of your brave bird

Now the world gossips
saying 'This is wrong'
O Tirumāl such is the fate of our precious girl.

88

She Said:

The great Meru is like Tirumāl
the red sun rising above that beautiful mountain
Tirumāl's hand holding the auspicious disc

When we see all that is like him
when we see his emblems his form
we stand entranced.
How can evil fate touch us
who worship Tirumāl?

89

She Said:

Poison to evil fate sweetest nectar to virtue
beloved of the goddess whose seat is a lotus
strapping cowherd who grazed his cows
thinking nothing of it

that day measured worlds
with his two feet
bull-like lord my master
when will we be united?

90

She Said:

I edged close to you
my desire to bear your feet on my head
a protection against this body

what a wonder is this body
I received as a reward for my many vows.
O my lord who destroyed the clan of demons
when I think on this
even the ancient aeon shrinks.

91

She Said:

The cunning one ate butter stored in pots
then swallowed the entire world whole
what a large belly he has

As a great dwarf he made a pact with Mahābali
for three steps of land
this servant's heart desires none
but the great wily lord.

92

She Said:

The gods begged you to raze
the wicked demon's great city
surrounded by wide ocean
They worship your feet that touched this earth

but do they think night and day
on at least one of your many forms?

93

She Said:

The night fled the sun in the morning
the sun dies the night returns
the wicked evening spreads everywhere

Even seeing this no one
bathes in the morning in the pond of knowledge
their bud-like eyes closed or open
they don't sing praises of Māl
they don't think of his dark body.

94

Virtuous Vedic seers
are blessed to be adorned by
your dark body your red lotus eyes your feet.

Like a blind cow mimicking the lowing herd
so it can return to the city
I repeat some words.
What else can this servant say?

95

She Said:

The soul enters a body
bound there then released
it falters in all its previous lives.

I want to be rid of this attachment
I worship Tirumāl
who is mother and father
the one who can grant me release.

96

She Said:

You created many places of pilgrimage
You created many religions different from each
For each of those religions you created gods

You spread your form everywhere
You have no equal
I awaken my desire for you.

97

She Said:

People are born they die
again and again aeon after aeon
seeing this don't they desire its end?

For those who love him feast their eyes on him
        that ancient Māl worshipped
        by the crowd of unblinking celestials
        who throng around him
Will their eyes ever close in sleep?

98

She Said:

The sages who don't sleep, all those others
who worship him constantly
wanting to end the pain of endless births
even the unblinking ones

can't understand the simple words
'He ate butter'
Peerless lord
of great singular form.

99

These may be simple words. But this is the good I've seen
There is only the master of knowledge
that one who took the form of a boar
lifted the world submerged in crashing waves.

Neither for the gods
who possess the great tree of wishes
nor for all the others
is there anyone else.

100

Mār̲an̲ who wears as a garland

the feet of those who recite Tirumāl's divine names
that lord of Kurukūr where good people
praise him

sang a plea of one hundred verses

those who master them
won't ever be trapped in the quicksand
of delusory birth its wicked fate
the misery of this false world.

PART II

THE MEASURE OF TIME

On Reading Nammāḻvār's *Tiruviruttam*

False wisdom wicked conduct dirty bodies
let's not draw near such things now

To protect life
you took birth from many wombs

O master of the unblinking ones

stand before me embodied
listen graciously to a servant's plea.[1]

Tiruviruttam 1

If Śaṭhakōpaṉ-Nammāḻvār's monumental *Tiruvāymoḻi* begins in a suitably monumental fashion speculating on the unfathomable nature of god, the more modest *Tiruviruttam*'s opening salvo is muted, humble and direct. The first verse sets forth the devotee's plea (*viṇṇappam*) to the supreme deity who, like in the *Tiruvāymoḻi*'s first decads, remains unnamed.[2] The request so innocently put forth in *Tiruviruttam* 1 is nothing less than a ravenous savouring of the mutual experience of union. God must heed—nay, graciously listen to—the devotee's account of the singular ecstasy of divine union. The poem itself is the viṇṇappam, as much a long, beautiful love letter to the divine as it is an abject request for grace. To see god in embodied form is to receive grace. For god to listen to the account of their spectacular love is to receive grace. To love god and to be loved by god is to receive grace. In the *Tiruviruttam*'s philosophical universe, divine grace is inseparable from divine love, and the absence of that love marks the absence of grace.

Nammāḻvār is not unique among bhakti poets in seeing grace and love as the other's mirror, but the *Tiruviruttam* stands out for its experimental meditation on these twin principles. The opening and closing verses act as the frame (the viṇṇappam) that encloses the poem's narrative heart: the developing love affair between an anonymous hero (*talaivaṉ*) and the heroine (*talaivi*). It charts the troughs and peaks of this epic love as witnessed by stock characters familiar to anyone who has read Indian love poetry: the hero, the heroine, the mother, friends, messengers and fortune tellers parade through the poem remarking on this treacherous love that has no end. But despite being bound by its formal structure—it is an *antāti*—and by the narrative logic of a developing love affair, the *Tiruviruttam* defies easy allegorical concordances. While it may not have achieved the iconic status of the *Tiruvāymoḻi*, this complex, provocative poem of hundred verses stands as a testament to the poetic and philosophical brilliance of Nammāḻvār.

The Poet: Śaṭhakōpaṉ-Nammāḻvār

Māṟaṉ who wears as a garland

the feet of those who recite Tirumāl's divine names
that lord of Kurukūr where good people praise him

sang a plea of one hundred verses

those who master them
won't ever be trapped in the quicksand
of delusory birth its wicked fate
the misery of this false world.

Tiruviruttam 100

The poet Śaṭhakōpan̲ is revered as the most important of the twelve *āḻvār* poets, those twelve foundational figures of the Śrīvaiṣṇava *saṁpradāya*s who lived in the Tamil-speaking regions of south India between the sixth and ninth centuries. He is so beloved to the Śrīvaiṣṇava communities that he comes to be addressed fondly as Nammāḻvār (Our Āḻvār).[3] This intimacy in no way diminishes his extraordinary consequence, for he is also venerated as the Śrīvaiṣṇavas' first *ācārya* (teacher), and his four compositions are equated to the four Vedas; within this schema, the *Tiruviruttam*, regarded as his first work, is equated to the *Ṛg Veda*. In keeping with his exalted place, Nammāḻvār's works, in particular the *Tiruvāymoḻi* and to a lesser extent the *Tiruviruttam*, have attracted concentrated study, deep contemplation and innumerable commentaries over the past 900 years.

Despite Nammāḻvār's central place in the development of the Śrīvaiṣṇava traditions, we know virtually nothing of his life. Shrouded in legend and mystery, Nammāḻvār emerges in the hagiographical literature as a highly evolved sage, the emanation of Viśvaksena, Viṣṇu's commander-in-chief on earth.[4] The story goes:

Viṣṇu took birth as the child of a devout Vēḷḷāḷa couple, but when the child was born, he neither cried nor spoke nor ate. After ten days of this odd behaviour, the despairing parents took the child to Kurukūr and left him under a tamarind tree. The infant crawled into a groove in the tree and went into a deep, silent meditation that lasted sixteen years. In his sixteenth year, a Brahmin devotee named Maturakavi followed a divine light that led him to the meditating youth. Astonished at the stillness of this boy, Maturakavi cast a stone at him to determine whether he was conscious. When the meditating sixteen-year-old opened his eyes, Maturakavi posed a riddle: 'If the small thing is born in the belly of a dead thing, what will it eat and where will it lie?' The boy answered obliquely, 'It will eat that and it will lie there.'[5] Maturakavi was delighted that he had found his teacher at last. The young boy, who was none other than Nammāḻvār, broke his silence and poured out his intense enjoyment of the divine in four compositions, of which the *Tiruviruttam* was the first and the *Tiruvāymoḻi* the last. As indicated by the final decad of the *Tiruvāymoḻi*, Nammāḻvār attained his heart's desire and was united with Viṣṇu.[6] In ritual performance tradition, Nammāḻvār's disappearance from this earth caused such distress to his devotees that Viṣṇu returned him to earth to act as a guide to all beings.[7]

While the story of Nammāḻvār's encounter with Maturakavi speaks of his singular character among the āḻvār poets—a silent seer who contributes more than a quarter of the four thousand verses of the *Nālāyira Divya Prabandham*—his later intervention in the recovery of the Vaiṣṇava canon expresses his unique place as a mediator par excellence. In this latter story, the *Tiruvāymoḻi* has been lost and Nāthamuni (c. tenth century), the first Śrīvaiṣṇava preceptor, seeks to restore this extraordinary composition to the world. He prays to Nammāḻvār, reciting Maturakavi's panegyric to his teacher over and over again. Impressed by Nāthamuni's single-minded devotion, Nammāḻvār appears before him and reveals the *Tiruvāymoḻi* as well as the composition of the remaining āḻvār poets. In this manner, Nammāḻvār is held to be crucial in reconstituting the lost *Divya Prabandham*, the Tamiḻ Veda.[8]

Such legendary events aside, the historical information on Nammāḻvār is scant. From the concluding *phala śruti* verses of his compositions, we know that he referred to himself as Śaṭhakōpaṉ and that he hailed from the town of Kurukūr, a town on the banks of the swift-flowing Thamiraparani. Located in the heart of southern Pāṇṭiya territory, this town was a wealthy place of fertile fields and virtuous Vaiṣṇavas. Although today Kurukūr is a small, sleepy village, Nammāḻvār portrays it as a grand, fortified city of ancient fame, intimately connected to its Pāṇṭiya legacy, one which he invokes in the phala śruti through the common Pāṇṭiya epithets Māṟaṉ, Kārimāṟaṉ and Vaḻuti, which tantalizes us with a plausible connection between him and the region's Pāṇṭiya rulers. He also describes himself as the king (*kōṉ*) of Kurukūr (for example, *Tiruvāymoḻi* III.6.11). Maturakavi's short eleven-verse composition *Kaṇṇiṉuṇ Ciṟu Tāmpu* (The Short Knotted String), in praise of Nammāḻvār, would appear to support Nammāḻvār's claims as a member of the political elite of Kurukūr. Maturakavi lauds Śaṭhakōpaṉ as the lord (*nampi*) and master (*pirāṉ*) of Kurukūr, and as Kārimāṟaṉ, the son of Kāri. This Kāri (Nammālvār's father) was possibly a Pāṇṭiya functionary in the region.[9]

Given the paucity of historically verifiable information, it is no surprise that Nammāḻvār's dates are disputed, and scholars place him anywhere between the late seventh and mid-ninth centuries. The Śrīvaiṣṇava saṁpradāyas take the

Bhāgavata Purāṇa's 'prophecy' of the coming of the āḻvār poets seriously, and use it to date them from 4200 BCE to 2700 BCE, placing their birth at the beginning of the Kali Yuga.[10] Alkondavilli Govindacharya, in an attempt to link Nammāḻvār's birth with the *Bhāgavata Purāṇa* and, more specifically, with the life of Kṛṣṇa, reports in his *Holy Lives of the Azhvars or the Dravida Saints* that Nammāḻvār was 'born just 43 days after the exit of Lord Krishna from the stage of this world'.[11] As devotion to the āḻvārs in general and Nammāḻvār in particular gathers steam during the time of Rāmānuja (1017–1137 CE, traditional dates), the theory of the *aṁśa* (emanation) comes to dominate conceptions of the āḻvārs' relationship to Viṣṇu. They are no longer just special, inspired poets, but are now Viṣṇu's emanations. With this new emergent framework and befitting his status as the chief among the āḻvār poets, Nammāḻvār is seen as a manifestation of Viśvaksena, Viṣṇu's chief attendant.[12]

Traditionally, Nammāḻvār is the fifth āḻvār, a position reflected in Vedānta Deśika's (1269–1370 CE) list of ten āḻvārs—he omits Āṇṭāḷ and Maturakavi.[13] But the *Rāmānuja Nūṟṟantāti*, a panegyric to the Śrīvaiṣṇavas' most important ācārya included in the *Nālāyira Divya Prabandham*, appears to place Nammāḻvār and Maturakavi at the end of the list.[14] The *Nūṟṟantāti* devotes a verse each to each of the twelve āḻvār beginning with Poykaiyāḻvār in verse 8 and ending with Nammāḻvār in verse 19. The *Rāmānuja Nūṟṟantāti* is concerned with tracing the lineal descent of the Śrīvaiṣṇava saṁpradāya, which continues after Nammāḻvār down to Nāthamuni (verse 20), Yāmunācārya (verse 21), and then eventually Rāmānuja. Nammāḻvār's place in the *Nūṟṟantāti* may reflect the tradition's emerging sense of chronology, where he is seen as the last āḻvār in order to establish the continuity of the tradition from Nammāḻvār down to Rāmānuja. This would account for placing Maturakavi ahead of Nammāḻvār, whom the poem evokes only in the most oblique fashion.

Earnest efforts to date the āḻvār begin in the early twentieth century, and initial academic estimates placed the twelve poet-saints after the period of Rāmānuja, hence mid-twelfth century.[15] These dates have long since been dismissed and most scholars agree that the āḻvār span a period of about 300 years, from 600 to 900 CE.[16] Where Nammāḻvār falls in this rather broad swathe of time is still a largely unresolved question. Scholars have used the same body of minimal sources—references to two temples sites in the *Tiruvāymoḻi* and another inscription from Madurai with the name Māṟaṉ Kāri—to draw wildly divergent conclusions for Nammāḻvār's date.

An inscription from Anamalai near Madurai describes the excavation of a Viṣṇu shrine sponsored by a Pāṇṭiya minister Māṟaṉ Kāri also known as Maturakavi.[17] The date on the inscription (Kali Year 3871) corresponds to 770 CE and coincides with the reign of the Pāṇṭiya king Parāntaka (also mentioned in the inscription). Gopinatha Rao draws several interesting, albeit somewhat far-fetched, conclusions based on this inscription, and dates Nammāḻvār to the early ninth century identifying the Parāntaka of the inscription with Jaṭila Parāntaka Neṭuñcaṭaiyaṉ also known as Varaguṇa I (756–815 CE). He proposes that based on the similarity of names, Nammāḻvār (who refers to himself as Kārimāṟaṉ) was the son of the minister in this inscription (Māṟaṉ Kāri). Then, somewhat implausibly, Rao suggests that Śaṭhakōpaṉ's father was a dynastic minister, serving under Parāṅkuśa Pāṇṭiya (also known as Arikesari Parāṅkuśa Māṟavaraman, 670–700 CE) and then his great-grandson Parāntaka Varaguṇa Pāṇṭiya. This might explain how Nammāḻvār comes to be known as Parāṅkuśa, a name that Rao suggests was given by the king's loyal minister to his son. In this same manner of passing on a family name (Māṟaṉ [grandfather] ⟶ Kāri-Maturakavi [father] ⟶ Māṟaṉ-Parāṅkuśa-Nammāḻvār [son]), Nammāḻvār's disciple is initiated with the name Maturakavi. Such contortionist logic allows Gopinatha Rao to reject the notion that the Maturakavi/Māṟaṉ Kāri identified in the Anamalai inscription is identical to Nammāḻvār's devoted pupil. Given that Nammāḻvār's father must have served his two kings in the late eighth century, and his son born sometime during this period, leads Rao to speculate on a date in the early ninth century for the poet.[18]

Vaiyapuri Pillai marshals a range of sources to make a case for a late-ninth-century date for Nammāḻvār. He dates the shrine of Varagunamangai mentioned in the *Tiruvāymoḻi* to the mid to late ninth century based on its name (honouring a Pāṇṭiya king named Varaguṇavarman II, 862–885 CE)[19] and on corroborative epigraphical information. He assigns Nammāḻvār a post-800 date, and goes so far as to propose placing him around 870 CE, making him roughly contemporaneous with Periyāḻvār and Āṇṭāḷ.[20] Vaiyapuri Pillai also sees several parallels in the unusual grammatical usages shared between Māṇikkavācakar's *Tiruvācakam* and the *Tiruvāymoḻi*, and between his *Tirukkōvaiyār* and the *Tiruviruttam*. He concludes (on tangential linguistic evidence) that Māṇikkavācakar slightly predates Nammāḻvār and fairly confidently assigns the Vaiṣṇava poet to post-875 CE.[21]

Krishnaswami Aiyangar rejects the late-ninth-century date proposed by Vaiyapuri Pillai (they have a long-standing feud by the time Aiyangar's *Early History of South Indian Vaishnavism* is published in 1920) on the basis of inscriptional and philological evidence. In fact, Aiyangar dismisses Nammāḻvār's mention of the temple site of Varagunamangai—a keystone of Vaiyapuri Pillai's dating—as a reliable means to fixing him as a contemporary of the king Varaguṇa Pāṇṭiya (862–885 CE).[22] In the end, Aiyangar proposes a somewhat improbable date of the fifth century for Nammāḻvār based on the fact that '*bhaktas*, both of Vishnu and Śiva were coming into prominence, and when the work of these *bhaktas* was beginning to tell upon those people that were following the persuasion of the Buddha and the Jina'.[23]

Wading in several decades after the intense debate between Pillai and Aiyangar, B.V. Ramanujam refutes many of Rao's deductions, but ultimately agrees with his dating. He finds Rao's links between Nammāḻvār and the king Parāṅkuśa Pāṇṭiya to be tenuous at best. Nammāḻvār does not refer to himself by the name/title Parāṅkuśa in his works; it is an epithet bestowed upon him much later. Also, it is far-fetched to assume that Nammāḻvār initiated his student with an epithet/name of his father, Maturakavi.[24] Nonetheless, Ramanujam finds the inscriptional evidence of the site Varagunamangai and the copper plates of Parāntaka I (756–815 CE) compelling, and agrees with Rao's estimation of an early-ninth-century date for Nammāḻvār and Maturakavi. His final conclusion is that Nammāḻvār and Maṭurakavi are in fact the last of the āḻvār poets.[25]

The art historian R. Nagaswamy derives a late-eighth-century date for Nammāḻvār from the epigraphical record of the two temples mentioned in the *Tiruvāymoḻi*, Srivaramangalam and Varagunamangai. Both sites are dated to the reign of Varaguṇa I (756–815 CE), that is, Parāntaka I. He corroborates this evidence against the two titles of the Pāṇṭiya king Arikesari Parāṅkuśa Māṟavarman (650–700 CE), suggesting, like Gopinatha Rao, that Nammāḻvār's titles Parāṅkuśa and Māṟaṉ honour this king.[26] He concludes that Nammāḻvār was possibly born around 745 CE but no later than 780 CE. Nagaswamy's date would make Nammāḻvār a contemporary of Tirumaṅkaiyāḻvār, who is generally dated to the same period on account of his reference to Nandivarman Pallavamalla's (731–796 CE) Parameśvara Viṇṇakaram temple in Kancipuram, now known as Vaikuntha Perumal temple.

Friedhelm Hardy infers a seventh- to early-eighth-century date for Nammāḻvār based on the influence of the first three āḻvār, particularly in his use of the antāti form, the sharpening of the use of the *akam* content in his poetry (something largely absent from the poetry of the earlier āḻvār poets), and the greater number of Vaiṣṇava temples mentioned.[27] Kamil Zvelebil, on the other hand, guided by Vaiyapuri Pillai's hypothesis, dates Nammāḻvār and his disciple Maturakavi as the last of the āḻvār poets. He draws his conclusions from the same inscriptional evidence provided by the same two late-eighth/early-ninth-century Viṣṇu shrines of Srivaramangalam and Varagunamangai. Finally, Nammāḻvār's close association to Nāthamuni in the Śrīvaiṣṇava hagiographic traditions leads Zvelebil to assign him to the period 880–930 CE.[28] Given the dearth of evidence and despite all the rigorous debates, it is unsurprising that we are unable to conclusively date this most important of āḻvār poets. At the most, we can reasonably assert that he and his student lived between the mid-eighth and the mid-ninth centuries.

Marking Time, Making Stories: The Structure of the *Tiruviruttam*

She Said:

The masters of the earth cleave
to the weighty words of the Ṛg Veda
to praise faultlessly
the feet that spanned the worlds

I depressed subdued by fate
simply recite sacred names I've learned
like one who can't eat ripe fruit
and makes do with raw ones.

Tiruviruttam 64

The *Tiruviruttam* is included in the Iyaṟpā section of the *Nālāyira Divya Prabandham* and keeps company with both the earliest and latest of the āḻvār compositions.[29] The *Tiruviruttam* follows the four works of Poykai, Pēy, Pūtam and Tirumaḻicai, and in its placement as the fifth poem of the Iyaṟpā invokes Nammāḻvār's traditional position as the fifth āḻvār. So although the entire *Divya Prabandham* is not organized chronologically but generically, the Iyaṟpā appears to be attentive to issues of chronology, form and content. Of the Iyaṟpā's ten compositions (sometimes eleven, depending on where we include the *Rāmānuja Nūṟṟantāti*), six use the antāti format, while the three poems of Tirumaṅkai (*Ciṟiya Tirumaṭal*, *Periya Tirumaṭal* and *Tiruveḻukūṟṟirukkai*) and the *Tiruviruttam* play with unusual content. The Iyaṟpā is the place for the experimental and the novel, whether represented in the ground-breaking poetry of the first three ā_lvār or in the poetic innovations of the master poet, Tirumaṅkai.[30] The inclusion of Nammā_lvār's *Tiruviruttam* in the Iya_rpā is both apt and deliberate, inviting the attentive reader to follow the development of poetic and philosophic ideas germane to the Śrīvaiṣṇava traditions.

The *Tiruviruttam*'s hundred interlinked verses are composed in the *viruttam* metre. A metre popular among the Tamil bhakti poets, it appears to have developed out of the old metres such as *kali* and *akaval*.[31] The word *viruttam* is derived from the Sanskrit *vṛtta*, which is used to denote metre in general, specifically those based on the number of syllables as opposed to syllable length and duration. Viruttam is also closely allied with a specific interpretive musical performance style. In performance and indeed in its wide application in Tamil poetry, the viruttam is used to underline the thrust of the narrative.[32] Śrīvaiṣṇava commentators' notes on the meaning of the poem's title *Tiruviruttam* are attentive to several interpretive possibilities. Deriving viruttam from *vṛtta/vṛttāntam* (event; that which occurred; news), they read the *Tiruviruttam* as reporting the events of Nammā_lvār's experience of union with and separation from Viṣṇu. For these commentators, the text is a synopsis of the ideas presented in the *Tiruvāymo_li*, while simultaneously it is the *means* through which one apprehends Nammā_lvār's mystical experience. As there is only one supreme man (*Puruṣottama*), all other sentient beings are inherently female. Therefore, the *Tiruviruttam* follows the familiar trajectory of a love story between Viṣṇu and his beloved. Within this paradigm, Viṣṇu is the lover and Nammā_lvār, in his female persona—the Parāṅkuśa Nāyikā—is his beloved. So the *Tiruviruttam* is interpreted as the record (vṛtta) of the woman's (*tiru*) enjoyment of Viṣṇu. Furthermore, as all women are Lakṣmī, it follows that the heroine of Nammāḻvār's poem is as beautiful (tiru) and inseparable from Viṣṇu as Lakṣmī (Tiru).

The *Tiruviruttam* is a beautifully constructed poem. Apart from the viruttam metre, its other formal feature is that of Nammāḻvār's favoured antāti, where the last syllable or word of one verse becomes the first word or syllable of the verse that immediately follows it. The antāti effectively links the words and verses together in a cycle, where beginning and end are obscured, and the poem's non-linearity opens up endless interpretive possibilities. Such interpretive capaciousness owes itself to the flexibility of the antāti itself—the *col-antāti* repeats the word; the *poruḷ-antāti* employs implied meaning; the *col(ṟ)-poruḷ antāti* interlinks through both form and content. Two verses from midway through the *Tiruviruttam* serve as an excellent illustration of Nammāḻvār's use of the antāti. Below I provide the transliterated Tamil text (with the *sandhi* deconstructed into individual words) and the English translations for the selected verses, *Tiruviruttam* 56 and 57. The antāti in Tamil is marked in bold.

viyaliṭam uṇṭapirāṉar viṭutta tiruvaruḷāl
uyal iṭam peṟṟu uyantam añcalam tōḻi ōr taṇ teṉṟal vantu
ayaliṭai yārum aṟintilar am pūntuḻāyiṉ iṉ tēṉ
puyaluṭai nīrmaiyiṉāl taṭaviṟṟu eṉ ***pulaṉka****laṉē*

Tiruviruttam 56

pula-k-k*uṇṭala-p-puṇṭarikatta pōr-k-keṇṭai valli oṉṟāl*
vilakkkuṇṭu ulākiṉṟu vēl viḻikkiṉṟaṉa kaṇṇaṉ kaiyāl

malakkuṇṭu amutam curanta ma<u>r</u>i kaṭal pō<u>nr</u>u ava<u>rr</u>āl
kalakkuṇṭa nā<u>nr</u>u kaṇṭār emmai yārum ka<u>l</u>a<u>r</u>alarē.

Tiruviruttam 57

She Said:

Beautiful friend don't be afraid
we survived because of the grace
of the lord who swallowed this wide world

a breeze cool as a rain cloud
came bearing the sweet fragrance of lovely tulasī
it caressed **my senses my jewels**
but no one else knows.

Tiruviruttam 56

He Said:

Her **earrings entrance the senses**.
In her lotus-like face her dark eyes dart like keṇṭai
whose war is blocked by a gently curving creeper
such eyes: wide and sharp as spears.

No one can mock me. Those eyes
bewilder me
I am like the ocean with its crashing waves
giving up its nectar
when Kaṇṇa<u>n</u> churned it with his mountain.

Tiruviruttam 57

The antāti between 56 and 57 replicates the sound and the word, but uses both with such inventiveness that the meaning subtly alters. *Tiruviruttam* 56 ends with *pulaṅ kalaṉē*, a compound of two words: *pulaṉ* (senses) and *kalaṉ* (ornaments/jewels). *Tiruviruttam* 57 begins with the phrase *pula-k-kuṇṭala(m)*, where the commentators read *pula* as a noun (*pulaṉ*, sense) or as an adjective (as beauty) that qualifies *kuṇṭalam* (earrings). In the latter case, the meaning is derivative—that which engages the senses (*pulaṉ*) is beautiful. With clever, implied wordplay as above, the poem is never boring or repetitive, despite the relatively constrictive character of the antāti. On a side note, Nammāḻvār's antāti is impossible to translate into English, largely because of his clever use of polyvalent words. Often, as is the case above, one has to expand the translated line to accommodate the polyvalence. So, in the translation, *taṭaviṟṟu eṉ pulaṅ kalaṉē* in *Tiruviruttam* 56 becomes 'caressed my senses, my jewels' and *pula-k-kuṇṭala* is rendered as 'her earrings entrance the senses'.

The antāti in the *Tiruviruttam* has another significant formal function, serving to bracket out its first and last verses, suggestively using the antāti to construct a framed narrative. *Tiruviruttam* 1 begins with the famous phrase *poy-niṉṟa jñāṉam* (false/illusory knowledge) and ends with *ceyyum viṇṇappamē* (the made petition/request). Given that this is an antāti, one would reasonably expect *Tiruviruttam* 2 to start with some syllabic or semantic variation of the first verse's final phrase, ***ceyyum*** *viṇṇappamē*. Nammāḻvār does not disappoint, and begins the second verse with the auspicious word ***ceḻu*** (abundant), which stands in stark opposition to the abject poy-niṉṟa jñāṉam that inaugurates the poem. The poem's final word in *Tiruviruttam* 100—the last word of the last verse—ends provocatively with *poy nilatē* (false state), a variation of *poy-ninra* which begins it, bringing the entire *Tiruviruttam* full circle.

At first glance, the *Tiruviruttam* is the tightly strung garland of words that it purports to be, fulfilling the mandate of its end-to-beginning antāti. But Nammāḻvār is a subtle, careful, deliberate poet, a master of the antāti. So when he deviates even slightly from the manner in which he generally employs the form, it demands our attention. By and large, when Nammāḻvār uses the antāti, he tends to repeat words or parts of words, either to assert a point or to insert a new one; ***poy*** *ni<u>nr</u>a* (1) and ***poy*** *nilam* (100) discussed above are exemplary of this technique. For instance, in the *Tiruviruttam*, the antāti linking verses 2, 3 and 4 all repeat some variation of the end-word of the preceding verse.[33] Thus the second verse's last word, *kuḻal* (curly hair), is mimicked as *kuḻal* (flute) in the third verse's first word; that verse ends with *ta<u>n</u>i neñcam* (lonely heart), which is reproduced exactly as the opening phrase of verse 4 (*ta<u>n</u>i neñcam*).

This system of repeated words (homonyms or otherwise) is in keeping with how the antāti typically works in all of Nammāḻvār's three antāti works: *Periya Tiruvantāti*, *Tiruvāymoḻi* and the *Tiruviruttam*. Indeed, the opening antātis of the *Periya Tiruvantāti* and the *Tiruvāymoḻi* carefully replicate sound and often the word as well, creating a cascade of tight visual and aural links. In this context then, the subtle, almost unnoticeable, break in the *Tiruviruttam*'s opening antāti is rendered all the more striking. Rather than using the formula that gets him through the majority of the *Tiruvāymoḻi* and the *Periya Tiruvantāti*, Nammāḻvār bypasses using the same word or a version of viṇṇappam or ceyyum, and instead chooses simply to replicate visually and aurally just the short first syllable (*ce*) of *ceyyum*, the penultimate word of verse 1, while still playing off the similar long vowel sound (*viṇṇappamē*) that brings the verse to a close. In principle, the antāti has not been violated, but in veering away from a tested and expected formula described above, the poet tricks us into hearing sounds that give the impression of an unbroken link.

Most obviously, the minor (perceived) break in the antāti allows the central action of the poem to begin on an auspicious note with an invocation of abundance (ceḻu) that nicely counteracts the wretched inauspiciousness of falseness and illusion that initiates it. In a sense, it permits the poem to begin twice, negating its false start. In doing so, Nammāḻvār sets up a frame and the pretext for the love story that permits the poet to make his petition, one that he requests Viṣṇu to listen to in his embodied, true form.[34] The deceptive antāti brackets out the main action of the poem even as he can inhabit the bodies and voices of his anonymous characters. It is a delightful sleight of hand that enables the *Tiruviruttam* to be simultaneously particular and universal. It *is* Nammāḻvār's story, his humble request, a record of his subjective experience. Yet the poem's nameless, cipher-like speakers become everyman, everywoman who desperately seek the lotus feet of Māl.

The connection between the poem's first and final verses can thus be seen only to evoke an impression, an approximation of continuity, alluding to the very state—delusion—that begins and ends the *Tiruviruttam*. The entire dramatic action takes place within the embrace of falseness, of *poymai*. It is within this womb of illusion, of *poy jñāṉam* (false knowledge) and *poy nilam* (false state) that the poem's hero and heroine fall in love, suffer, and eventually find a way out. By providing a frame by means of two (false) starts, the poem also signals its two levels of meanings. It is not *just* about an anonymous, ordinary love affair; that would be an illusion. The viṇṇappam (his poem), although addressed to Viṣṇu to listen graciously, may equally address us, exhorting us to listen with care, and cautioning us to be ever attentive to illusion.

The *Tiruvāymoḻi* too takes us on this path, via its seamless antāti but with equally dramatic juxtapositions. The *Tiruvāymoḻi*'s first verse, I.1.1, begins auspiciously with the word *uyar* (high) and ends with the intimate *maṉam* (heart-mind). Uyar, expressive of the supremacy and infinity of Viṣṇu's nature is set beside the intimate vastness of the devotee's own mind (maṉam). As Śrīvaiṣṇava commentators since the twelfth century have pointed out, the *Tiruvāymoḻi*'s unbroken antāti structure reflects a refined theology, one which articulates god's paradoxical nature, as one who is transcendent, yet resides in the devotee's heart-mind (maṉam).

The *Tiruviruttam* seeks to say something equally profound not only through the minor break between verses 1 and 2, but also in its constant subversion of the narrative it intends to unfold. Even as the antāti falters just as the poem begins, the story of the mystical love affair is already in full bloom. And as that affair intensifies, hitting the high notes of union and resonating with the keening cries of lamentation, it too falters. The characters—the heroine, the friend, the hero, the mother—are intermittently abandoned, the poem traverses a different path, and the poet speaks directly to us (to god?) as if to reveal the impossibility of his quest. As striking as the broken garland of words that begins the *Tiruviruttam* is the changeable, sporadically splintering love-frame, which is eventually completely abandoned as the poem approaches its conclusion. In the last ten verses, the poem switches registers with no warning, forsakes the lovelorn heroine and love-struck hero and turns to philosophical ruminations that seem more at home in the *Tiruvāymoḻi*. After roaming the dry deserts of loss and separation, we are back where we began, addressing a request to Viṣṇu directly without the artifice of dramatic personae. The quicksilver alterations in register and in voices, the illusory, almost-heard, almost-seen antāti gap in the *Tiruviruttam* widen into the gulf between reality and falsehood, between this world and Viṣṇu's heaven, between a world in which Viṣṇu stands before the devotee embodied and one in which the devotee is bereft.

Such persistent adjustments in register, the poem's raucous multivocality and its studied repetitions all conspire to produce an intentional ambiguity that generates disquiet. It might be said that willed interruption in its many *avatāra*s is the poem's defining characteristic. Wielded with subtlety and purpose, interruption speaks quietly and powerfully of the ephemeral, broken, unsustainable quality of the (Nammāḻvār's) mystical experience. It captures in pitch-perfect harmony the frenzied delight of union and the bewildering sense of loss that inevitably follows.

A Poetry of Interruptions: Reading the *Tiruviruttam*

Celestials in the sky
offer you pure perfect garlands anoint you with cool water
worship you with beautiful incense

you vanish by a trick

to scoop up and eat butter
to dance between the two sharp horns

of the humped bull
for the lovely woman of the strong cowherd clan.

Tiruviruttam 21

Despite its formal and thematic structure, the *Tiruviruttam* is a poem of fits and starts, of repeated beginnings and endings. The poem's two beginnings (verses 1 and 2), the heroine's frustrated desire and her fleeting unions with her divine lover Viṣṇu are the most obvious manifestations of such narrative disruptions. The poem's frequent recourse to specific motifs—the night stretching into an aeon is a favourite—its deliberate rejection of linear narrative action, the confusion between the poem's many speakers, and so on, are just some of the ways in which the *Tiruviruttam* enshrines interruption—or, perhaps more appropriately, disruption—as a definitive index of Nammāḻvār's experience of Viṣṇu.[35] So even while some of these rhetorical techniques are shared by like-minded poets like Āṇṭāḷ and Tirumaṅkai, the *Tiruviruttam* is singular and remarkable among āḻvār poems for the degree to which it concertedly discomfits the reader/listener.

Generations of Śrīvaiṣṇava commentators have attempted in their own unique way to make sense of this baffling poem, guided by the imperatives of emergent Śrīvaiṣṇava theology. In their reading, the poem unfolds along two intertwined tracks of meaning. The first level, known as *anyāpadeśa*, is the external, the 'other', lesser reading, while *svāpadeśa* refers to the poem's inner, esoteric meaning. Anyāpadeśa and svāpadeśa are entwined in the poem, śleṣa-like, holding several meanings in balance at once. Yet the *Tiruviruttam* is littered with verses that deliberately confound the dual anyā/svāpadeśa structure. There are purely svāpadeśa verses, profoundly introspective and meditative, accommodating no other register. There are anyāpadeśa verses such as those spoken in the hero's voice that obscure its svāpadeśa. Still other times, a purely svāpadeśa verse is injected without warning, upsetting the slow building dialectic of union and separation. *Tiruviruttam* 21 quoted above is one such example.

Although commentators identify *Tiruviruttam* 21 as spoken in the heroine's voice, it is also in fact the poem's first purely svāpadeśa verse. It follows a verse (*Tiruviruttam* 20) that recounts a conversation between the heroine's friend (*tōḻi*) and her mother (*tāy*) about the true cause of the girl's disease. Mimicking many a foolish, misguided Caṅkam poem-mother, here too she summons Murukaṉ's priest to exorcise her lovesick daughter. The clever friend intercedes: 'It is not the Vēlaṉ. Repeat the names of the one who swallowed the seven worlds. Adorn her with his garland' (*Tiruviruttam* 20).[36] As if taking this counsel to heart, *Tiruviruttam* 21 begins with a description of ritual services that the celestials offer Viṣṇu in the high heavens. But, more importantly, the verse sets up familiar contrasts between the transcendent and the accessible, between his formlessness and the beauty of his form, between the timelessness of his existence and an adoration of a specific moment in time. The celestials worship a form that is not described, while on earth he is lovingly described—here he is scooping up the butter, there he is dancing and wrestling the seven bulls all for the love of a cowherd woman. Indeed, *Tiruviruttam* 21 immediately calls up the famous verse from the *Tiruvāymoḻi* I.3.1, which highlights Viṣṇu's accessibility to his devotees:

> Accessible to those with love, for others hard to find,
> amazing, the lady in the lotus takes pleasure at his feet so
> hard for us to gain,

yet because he stole the churned butter, his waist was
bound—what?—
to the grindstone—how vulnerable![37]

Śrīvaiṣṇava commentaries write of Nammāḻvār swooning at this moment in the composition of the *Tiruvāymoḻi*, overcome by the image of Viṣṇu, that lord of gods, the one who abides in all things, allowing himself to be bound, to be confined by the love of his devotee. In *Tiruviruttam* 21, as if in response to the friend's well-considered advice, the poet evokes this very image of the mercurial lord, who vanishes by a trick to transform into the butter thief and the lover of the cowherd-woman. Periyavāccāṉ Piḷḷai, one of the earliest commentators on this verse, produces a long, detailed interpretation invoking the first three decads of the *Tiruvāymoḻi* as a point of reference: in *Tiruvāymoḻi* I.1, Viṣṇu is shown in his transcendent form; in I.2 Nammāḻvār establishes the *upāya*, the means to attain Viṣṇu; and finally in I.3 he demonstrates that because of his accessibility, most fully realized in the Kṛṣṇa avatāra, Viṣṇu is both the way and the means to the goal of *mokṣa*.[38] The unspoken message is of course that *this* heroine too will be graced in just such a manner, for that is Viṣṇu's nature. It will do us well to remember that the motif of the butter thief is invoked a mere five times but always at a crucial juncture in the *Tiruviruttam*, prompting the poet and his audience towards intimacy with Viṣṇu that the true (or even accidental) devotee can cultivate. And so it is that with *Tiruviruttam* 22 we revert to the poem's conceit, and order is seemingly restored. Our familiar characters return, the hero makes consecutive appearances in *Tiruviruttam* 22 and 23 as if to tighten the bolts of the poem's narrative machinery.

It would seem that a tentative resolution is at hand. While *Tiruviruttam* 21 disrupts our expectations by introducing an unexpected svāpadeśa verse, it also efficiently serves as a kind of self-commentary, alerting us to the poem's dual universe, one that mirrors Viṣṇu's twin realms. We can regard the intervening svāpadeśa verse not so much as an interruption but as a mediation guiding the poem's theological contours. Regardless of these half-solutions, the two dialogic verses that immediately follow *Tiruviruttam* 21 throw up a different set of problems, equally difficult to reconcile.

Tiruviruttam 22 and 23 reintroduce the hero (talaivan̲), who appears for the first time in *Tiruviruttam* 6 speculating about the heroine's identity. We know the heroine is already in love with Kaṇṇan̲ (*Tiruviruttam* 2), her love adorning his feet. By the time we come to *Tiruviruttam* 22 and 23 a relationship is flourishing between the hero and heroine, although the poem deliberately obfuscates the hero's relationship to Viṣṇu. The hero as he emerges in these early *Tiruviruttam* verses is a besotted, bewildered fool, struck dumb by love. In *Tiruviruttam* 22 and 23 he too arrives as if by a trick, pretending to have lost his way:

The Friend Said:

In your hand you hold a leafy branch
you have no bow with which to hunt
yet you inquire about an elephant
you shot

Sir in this wide world
of that thief who rides the bird

no one speaks such things.
Is it to answer your odd questions
that we are here in this vast grove?

Tiruviruttam 22

To her pointed questions—she has clearly seen through his pretence—the hero responds:

He Said:

I was passing by this grove.
My fate is terrible.
O women, tell me if you guard
my heart or this grove?

O you with eyes the colour
of a beautiful lotus grove
O you who are equal to the gods
who live in Kaṇṇaṉ's celestial city!
Is this your nature?

Tiruviruttam 23

The Śrīvaiṣṇava commentators have a long tradition of reading the *Tiruviruttam* through allegoresis. Each character in the *Tiruviruttam* becomes something or someone else. The heroine is the soul, the friend is the mediator, the mother counsels patience, and so forth. But the *Tiruviruttam*'s hero presents a unique problem for the traditional commentator, for he appears in the poem not just as the silent object of the heroine's desire, as in the *Tiruvāymoḻi*, but as an active speaker and actor, who too desires the heroine. Reading the hero as Viṣṇu in the former situation is almost an instinctive move for the Śrīvaiṣṇava commentators. Indeed, the *Tiruviruttam* encourages such a reading, making it clear from its outset that the object of the heroine's desire is Viṣṇu: 'her love (*aṉpu*) adorns the feet / of Kaṇṇaṉ dark as heavy rain clouds' (*Tiruviruttam* 2). Yet when the hero speaks for the first time in *Tiruviruttam* 6, despite the precedent set by Rāma's longing for Sītā in the Rāmāyaṇa and Periyavāccāṉ Piḷḷai's love for that text, the hero is not identified as Viṣṇu. Let us look at *Tiruviruttam* 6:

He Said:

Who is this girl
eyes broad as arrows
brows curved like bows
whose shy glance retreats from improper things
a gently swaying creeper?

She is death
mastered by the sceptre of the one
who destroys demons
who rides that swift bird
whose son is sweet Madana
Shelter your life in this world.

Periyavāccāṉ Piḷḷai offers both an anyāpadeśa and svāpadeśa reading of the verse.[39] In the anyāpadeśa reading, *Tiruviruttam* 6 is the first introduction of the hero as an active desiring agent, and the mutual love of the hero and heroine. According to classical Tamil love poetics such a verse constitutes the hero's initial vision of the heroine known as the *nalam parāṭṭu* (a panegyric to virtues) or the *kāṭci makiḻtal* (joy at the vision). It occurs under the broad category of *iyaṟkai-p-puṇarcci* which in itself has several sub-stages: *kāṭci* (vision), *aiyam* (doubt), *tuṇivu* (realizing the heroine's human identity) and finally *kuṟippaṟital* (recognizing their mutual love).[40] Customarily, the hero who finds himself in this situation is stunned by the heroine's beauty and proceeds to sing her praises. Following the poetic conventions, Periyavāccāṉ Piḷḷai tells us the hero is drawn to the young woman's modesty evident in the manner in which her eyes withdraw from all improper things and by her creeper-like form, which indicates her dependency.[41] These subtle moments in Piḷḷai's anyāpadeśa reading of the verse set up the brief discussion of its svāpadeśa. The speaker of the poem is no longer Viṣṇu, but assembled *bhāgavata*s praising Nammāḻvār whose closed eyes look inward, having drawn away from all that is improper in this world.[42] This is of course in keeping with the petition that the poet himself sets out at the poem's commencement—let us not draw near filthy bodies and illusory thinking. Piḷḷai's analysis of the hero's voice in *Tiruviruttam* 6 guides how he proceeds to interpret these specific verses through the course of the poem. So it is unsurprising that Periyavāccāṉ Piḷḷai offers up the following succinct svāpadeśa summation for the hero's words in *Tiruviruttam* 23: the words of the Vaiṣṇavas upon observing Nammāḻvār's love for Viṣṇu's eternal realm (*nitya vibhūti*). Interpretive gymnastics notwithstanding, the *Tiruviruttam*'s capacious structure encourages a range of possibilities, allowing both Viṣṇu and Nammāḻvār to become objects of desire.

Same Day Madness: Endings and Beginnings in the *Tiruviruttam*

She Said:

The reign of the blazing sun who alone rules the
sky ended.
Cool dark night spreads through the world.
Who can stop the cool breeze that comes bearing
tulasī
to stoke a love that brings only misery?

Who will protect my bangles?
O this aeon ravages me!

Tiruviruttam 13

Time, as metre and as memory, looms large in the *Tiruviruttam*. Time in its formal guises neatly circumscribes experience through regulated metrical feet, proper head-rhymes and the stern demands of the antāti. The poem's dialogic moments tantalize with the possibility of narrative linearity, a linearity that sits uncomfortably with the autobiography Śrīvaiṣṇava commentators seek in the poem. In contradistinction, the poem's distinctive antāti evokes cyclical time, *saṁsāra* itself, endless and repetitive time that grasps the speaker/Nammāḻvār with unrelenting sureness. The significance of time is set out in the very first verse of the *Tiruviruttam*, which repeats some form of the verb *nil* (to stay/to stand) once in each of its four lines. In the first two lines the poet uses it (as *ni<u>nr</u>a*) to convey a static, habitual rootedness, of being unable to find a way out of the morass of evil deeds, false knowledge and filthy bodies. In the verse's final two lines, *nil* in its adjectival and adverbial forms is applied to Viṣṇu, and it immediately invokes movement, action and intervention. Viṣṇu the giver of life is praised as the one who took birth in many wombs. The irony is of course rich. Here is the poet caught in the filth of his own birth, desperately seeking a way out. And there is the god who gives life, takes birth and remains beyond it all. Mediating these two moments, these two worlds of these two beings, is the phrase ***iṉi*** *yām uṟāmai*—let us not draw near (all that) **henceforth**. As the devotee distances himself from an embodied life—no longer, he says—he petitions the god of many births to stand before him in true, embodied form (*mey-n-niṉṟu*) to listen. The crux of the *Tiruviruttam* lies here: the poem through both interruption and repetition continually reproduces the discomfort of living in saṁsāra, the sense that you live this life over and over again. Life might appear to follow a linear trajectory, moving in one direction from birth to death, until something disrupts that quiet acceptance, until one suddenly awakens to say: henceforth we stay away from wicked deeds and illusory knowledge.

The *Tiruviruttam* systematically develops the theme of awakening and coming alive to Viṣṇu's presence through the clever and judicious use of particular motifs and metaphors. One striking example will make the point sufficiently. As its very title suggests, the *Tiruviruttam* is concerned with time—the time that we live in this world and the use we make of that time. Iṉi yām uṟāmai—no longer this attachment—is the poem's underlying, implied refrain. But even though desire has awakened, the time spent in this life cannot be arrested. It is through these eyes that we must approach the numerous verses about the night, which are scattered through the poem. The first occurrence is in *Tiruviruttam* 12 when the heroine says:

> My jewel-like lustre fades
> a thick dense paleness spreads all over me
> the night is an aeon
> and everything else is like this
>
> such is the special wealth
> bestowed upon my heart
> bonded to Kaṇṇaṉ's cool lovely tulasī
> my lord who wields the sharp disc.

The endless night is a common motif in Indic love poetry, intensifying the loneliness of the abandoned, waiting lover. Sleep eludes her and she can find no solace even in dreams. Instead, she keeps a long, lonely vigil awaiting the errant beloved's promised return. She is awake. Like those yogis who neither eat nor sleep (*Tiruviruttam* 66), who avoid even closing their eyes should they miss a single moment of enjoying Viṣṇu's glorious form (*Tiruviruttam* 97), she waits and watches, tormented by the night as it returns again and again, each time more terrible and more vicious. Its dense blackness blankets the world, obscures everything and stretches as an aeon, into a thousand aeons. *He*, on the other hand, slumbers peacefully on the rolling ocean through the aeons that are no more than a blink of an eye to him, almost unmindful of his young lover's misery, until he comes awake to eat the worlds. Eventually, as the night continues its relentless assault on the helpless heroine, she recognizes something important:

She Said:

O girl with lustrous brow
O girl equal to the earth that he
Madhusūdanan̲ Dāmodaran̲
great lord
whose tulasī garlands dark bees feed on
eats spits out protects

Listen:
I've encountered this swollen night before
but I've neither seen nor heard nor known
a night that spreads like this.

Tiruviruttam 49

In a moment of hyper awareness, the heroine recognizes the fatalism at the heart of her impossible situation. The coming of the night is as inevitable as the creation and dissolution of the world, and as long as we live in this world, inhabit this body and are estranged from Viṣṇu, the night is guaranteed to torment us.

The *Tiruviruttam*'s conclusion finally gets us precisely to this point. In fact, one might argue that *Tiruviruttam*'s resolution rests in its final decad of verses. In this final ten (and the eleventh, the phala śruti), the text's major themes, prominent motifs and dominant myths come together as the multiple personae (hero, heroine, friend, etc.) simply dissolve, subsumed into the ringing tones of the poem's speaker/ Nammāḻvār. In shedding these alternate skins and alternate voices, these artifices, the speaker-poet is suddenly no longer an abandoned, pitiable figure; he is guide and teacher. As such, this last decad acts as a delicate counterpoint to the vexations and privations of desire. If verse 1 tells us to reject the filthy body, verse 90 celebrates that very body as a means to serve Viṣṇu: 'What a wonder is this body / I received as a reward for my many vows.' The tormenting night is the villain of the text, remorseless in its pursuit of the day and of the hapless heroine. In verse 93 this very night is dismissed, cut to pieces as though by Rāma's mighty arrows.

She Said:

The night fled the sun in the morning
the sun dies the night returns
the wicked evening spreads everywhere

Even seeing this no one
bathes in the morning in the pond of knowledge.
their bud-like eyes closed or open
they don't sing praises of Māl
they don't think of his dark body.

All it takes is a dip in the 'pond of knowledge', to praise Māl, and the darkness of saṁsāra dissipates of its own volition. The thick darkness of the night transmutes into the glittering glory of Māl's dark form, but only to those willing to see. With open eyes, desire awakened and the body enlivened, the earnest petition of the opening verse transforms into revelation in *Tiruviruttam* 94. The poet is no more than a blind cow mimicking a lowing herd, reproducing words that he cannot understand, simply the vehicle through which Viṣṇu speaks and acts. As Nammāḻvār empties himself of his many voices, his many characters, and as his desire awakens, his beloved god dark as night spreads himself everywhere and becomes the only voice that matters. And so it is that when even the great sages and seers cannot understand how the supreme, world-striding Viṣṇu came to eat butter, Nammāḻvār implies that *he* understands (*Tiruviruttam* 98) because he has *seen*. The yogis may remain sleepless or meditative, but it is the poet who is privy to a vision of the divine form. The poet is careful to remind us of the intimate relationship between waking and seeing: this is the good I *saw*, he insists as he assures us of the veracity of his experience (*Tiruviruttam* 99). In the end, the frame dissolves itself and the experiences of the preceding ninety-seven verses are presented as direct apprehension. 'I *say* these simple, low words because *this* is the good I saw.' Presumably, the petition of the first verse has been fulfilled; Viṣṇu has listened to him in embodied form. No one exists but the master of knowledge (*jñāna-p-pirā<u>n</u>*) who defeats false knowledge just as easily as he dispatched the night.

Birthing a Genre: *Tiruviruttam* and *Tirukkōvaiyār*

The *Tiruviruttam* was not born in a vacuum. Several scholars—A.K. Ramanujan, Norman Cutler, Friedhelm Hardy and Indira Peterson chief among them—have explored the transformation of akam and *pu<u>r</u>am* modes of antecedent Caṅkam poetry into Tamil bhakti poetry.[43] In doing so, we have grown attentive to specific choices that the new devotional poets made: shifting the object of attention from the king to god, remaking the wandering bard into the itinerant devotee and, most significantly, melding the boundaries of the public world of kingship and ethics with the private realm of love and desire. The mark of the Caṅkam predecessors on these bhakti poets is unmistakable, whether they are recasting beloved tropes (the monsoon clouds or the conch bangles) or alluding to and reshaping specific Caṅkam poems. Nammāḻvār is himself well aware of his debt to these poets as are his commentators. *Tiruviruttam* 26 makes the debt explicit:

He Said:

> O girl like gold, you crossed this wasteland
> that the lovely fierce sun spat out
> when he swallowed the four lands
> and sucked them dry.
>
> Look! Just beyond Kaṇṇaṉ's Veḥkā
> where even gods come to pray
> lie lovely cool flower gardens rich with honey
> that give comfort no matter one's state.

Nammāḻvār opens the above verse with the phrase *nāṉ-nilam*, four lands, which evokes the foundational principle of Tamil poetics—that of the landscapes or *tiṇai*s. Belonging to the category of verse known as *nakar kāṭṭal* (gesturing to the city), *Tiruviruttam* 26 depicts a familiar situation. The lovers have eloped, crossed the wasteland, at last glimpsed civilization and the end to their troubles. Ever sensitive to his Caṅkam antecedents, Nammāḻvār utilizes the appropriate tiṇai, the *pālai* or wasteland, when he adopts the situation for his *Tiruviruttam*. While this in itself is not unique—we see our poet demonstrate his literary erudition frequently in the *Tiruvāymoḻi*—it is the manner in which he does so in this specific instance that sets *Tiruviruttam* 26 apart.[44] But what might appear at first glance to be an erroneous understanding of akam poetics (speaking of four lands instead of five) in fact reveals the poet's command of his literary past. In *Tiruviruttam* 26, the hero speaks of pālai as a land leached of life by a fiery sun. It is an idea expressed in the Tamil Jain epic *Cilappatikāram*. The poet Ilaṅkō Aṭikaḷ through the voice of a Brahmin interlocutor denies that pālai is a landscape all its own. Instead, the Brahmin says:

> You have come with your wife in the season
> When the forests and hills have shed their nature,
> Lost their fresh looks by taking the form
> Of a wasteland, thus causing great hardship.[45]

These words occur in a section called *kāṭu kāṇ kātai* (The Chapter on Seeing the Forest; lines 60–66) when the Tamil epic hero Kōvalaṉ and his wife, Kaṇṇaki, abandon their hometown of Pukār, and encounter a Brahmin en route to the city of Madurai. The idea of pālai as a 'situational desert' is not something distinctive to the *Cilappatikāram*, because according to commentators and the *Tolkāppiyam*'s *Poruḷatikāram*, there is no desert per se in Tamil country, and it is the fierce heat of summer that transforms an otherwise lush landscape into a wasteland.[46] Nammāḻvār not only employs the landscape and its attendant situation perfectly (pālai, elopement and the sighting of the city) but also does so by alluding to a moment in the *Cilappatikāram* that parallels the imagined circumstances of the apparently anonymous hero and heroine of the *Tiruviruttam*.[47] *Tiruviruttam* 26 is as much about Nammāḻvar demonstrating his formidable learning as it is about appropriating a Tamil Jain literary work to serve his own ends.

Such awareness of the literary past in the *Tiruviruttam* is not isolated. Indeed, I will argue below that the very structure of the poem anticipates the rich development of the *kōvai* genre in the deft hands of Māṇikkavācakar (late ninth century), and as such is itself influenced by the *Aiṅkuṟunūṟu*, one of the last great anthologies of Caṅkam love poetry (In a personal communication, David Shulman suggested that the *Tiruviruttam*, in its shifting frames, genres, modes, also anticipates the *kalampakam*, a later medieval genre.) The relatively late *Aiṅkuṟunūṟu* (third century) stands apart for its tight, deliberate organization—five sections of one hundred verses each dedicated to each of the five landscapes and composed by five different poets. Martha Selby argues that the *Aiṅkuṟunūṟu*'s five poets collaborated in service of their patron to produce a single work of five hundred verses meant to be read as such.[48] Each of the hundred-verse sections devoted to a specific landscape (tiṇai) is further subdivided into groups of tens, devoted to a specific theme, motif or idea: ten on crabs, ten of Toṇṭi town, ten of the water buffalo, and so on.

The division of a work into sets of ten is a recognizable organizational feature of Tamil bhakti poetry. The thematic tens of the *Aiṅkuṟunūṟu* can well be regarded as anticipating the *patikam* form that dominates bhakti poetry. The Śaiva *Tēvāram*s are set into patikams (literally, sets of ten) centred generally on a particular myth or sacred abode of Śiva, while its Vaiṣṇava counterpart is the *Tirumoḻi* (literally, Sacred Language), which also develops around set motifs, themes or sites.[49] Nammāḻvār's *Tiruvāymoḻi* is itself carefully planned into ten cycles of a hundred songs, which are further segmented into sets of ten that focus on special sites, themes or philosophical ideas. The *Tiruviruttam* has no such easily discernible structure, no neat sets of ten to guide our readings, except for the poem's final eleven verses (90–100) that do cohere around the poem's central motifs—the night, the divine vision, sleeping and wakefulness, and, finally, revelation. Nonetheless, the structure of the *Aiṅkuṟunūṟu* can tell us something of where we place the *Tiruviruttam* in Tamil literary history and how this might help us make sense of its curious structure.

The *Aiṅkuṟunūṟu*'s overarching concern is the development of love, but it reverses the traditional order of the tiṇais as articulated in the *Tolkāppiyam*. That is, the Caṅkam poem begins at the end, with domestic quarrel (*marutam*) and concludes with patient waiting after marriage (*mullai*). Martha Selby posits that this new order concerns a desire to conclude it on an auspicious note: 'In the *Aiṅkuṟunūṟu*, the landscapes move from poems about fracture, jealousy and infidelity and settle finally into verses describing and celebrating domestic romance.'[50] From this vantage, the *Aiṅkuṟunūṟu* is concerned not just with a sustained meditation on love but also in developing a *narrative* around it. Earlier Caṅkam verses (and this can be equally true of the *Aiṅkuṟunūṟu*) are composed as stand-alone pieces, largely independent of those that either follow or precede them. But each verse of the *Aiṅkuṟunūṟu*, through the judicious use of tiṇai, enfolds the entire love narrative into it, suggesting both the couple's past and the future. *Kuṟiñci* verses depicting the bloom of first love and its attendant anxieties equally evoke in their marutam guise the despair of marital love, quarrel and infidelity. What is merely suggestive in Caṅkam anthologies is more fully realized in the *Aiṅkuṟunūṟu*, which I propose paves the way for the development of narrative genres such as the kōvai.[51]

As a genre the kōvai unfurls the gradual but strictly governed development of love between a well-suited hero and heroine over four hundred verses. In the kōvai, love matures along specifically mandated poetic moments: the first vision, the questions of the heroine's antecedents, the first meeting, and so forth. It develops in the nexus of the Tamil poetic and grammatical tradition, as attested to in its exemplary use in Nakkīrar's famous commentary on *Iṟaiyaṉār Akapporuḷ* (fourth to fifth century). The incomplete *Pāṇṭikkōvai*, the earliest extant kōvai, forms an integral part of Nakkīrar's commentary, although only 329 verses of this text have survived. It is by far the most cited work in Nakkīrar's commentary, its 329 verses dwarfing the fifty citations from classical and late-classical Tamil works. Based on the hero of the poem, the Pāṇṭiya king Neṭumāṟaṉ, Takahashi dates the *Pāṇṭikkōvai* to between 670 and 775 CE, and thus Nakkīrar's commentary to around the eighth century.[52] One might reasonably argue that this hundred-year period saw a gradual conceptual shift in Tamil poetics and poetry, one that strung buds of stories into fully blooming narrative garlands.

Nammāḻvār's *Tiruviruttam* emerges at just this cusp, between the tantalizing suggestions of the *Aiṅkuṟunūṟu* and the full realization of a narrative genre such as the kōvai in the hands of the master Śaiva poet, Māṇikkavācakar. The adaptation of Caṅkam poetics thus goes well beyond bursting open the categories of akam and puṟam or in the creative intermingling of the tiṇais. The autobiographical, confessional quality of Tamil bhakti poetry readily lends itself to narrative exposition. To a poet like Nammāḻvār, heir to a rich literary past, a new genre like the kōvai might well prove attractive, to experiment with possibilities both philosophical and poetic, which necessitate adhering to not just one but two stringent formal elements: the antāti and the kōvai. Lest we forget, the *Tiruviruttam* is *not* a kōvai—it is not four hundred verses long and it does not follow the prescribed steps from clandestine love to quiet, domestic happiness. Nevertheless, like the kōvai, the poem does attempt to construct a narrative about how one falls in love. Not only are the stock characters summoned in service of an overarching narrative about a mortal/divine love affair, many of the kōvai elements such as those mentioned above are present. With no other organizing principle such as thematic tirumoḻis to hold it together, the love narrative becomes the poem's mortar. Even as the Śrīvaiṣṇava commentators uncover the poem's svāpadeśa, they readily acknowledge the imperative of the (autobiographical) love story. Of course the *Tiruviruttam*'s love story does not hold together, and the pretext is eventually abandoned when we are well into the poem. This is in no way a flaw in the poem, for its complexity, its haunting quality emerge from Nammāḻvār's extraordinary poetic sensibility and his attempt to remake a largely secular genre into a devotional one. In many ways the *Tiruviruttam*, even with its deliberately broken, disjunctive narrative can be seen as a proto-kōvai, domesticated to the needs of bhakti poetry; the *Tiruviruttam* is not just a precursor to the *Tiruvāymoḻi* but arguably also paves the way for the *Tirukkōvaiyār*.[53]

The *Tiruviruttam* and *Tirukkōvaiyār* may not at first glimpse appear to be a natural, complementary pair.[54] Not only is their composition separated by some years, the far longer *Tirukkōvaiyār* clocking in at four hundred verses adheres with steadfast vigour to the strictures of the kōvai genre, an attempt perhaps to reclaim Tamil poetry for Śaivism, as Norman Cutler has suggested.[55] The narratively nebulous, non-linear *Tiruviruttam*, addressed to Viṣṇu, stays true to a long tradition of āḻvār love poetry, and in its own way participates in the reconfiguring of the Tamil literary past to the imperatives of emergent Tamil bhakti.

In the Caṅkam poetic traditions the phases of love are divided broadly into two major categories: *kaḷavu* (secret love) and *kaṟpu* (marital love). Later Tamil poetic grammars such as *Nampiyakapporuḷ* (thirteenth century) identify thirty-two moments (*kiḷavi*) in the movement from love to marriage. Of these, seventeen kiḷavi concern secret love, while the remaining fifteen describe marriage and marital love.[56] In keeping with the demands of the kōvai genre, the *Tirukkōvaiyār* takes us from the first blush of love to the trials of marriage, whereas the *Tiruviruttam* remains preoccupied primarily with secret love (kaḷavu). The poem rarely takes us beyond love consummated in secret but shared spaces (the forest or the seashore) past the threshold of love domesticated through marriage (kaṟpu).[57] Apart from the elopement described in *Tiruviruttam* 26 and 37, the poem seems set on deferring union. Obstacles to the lovers' union rarely come in the guise of the courtesan, in petty domestic quarrelling or in the pursuit of wealth after marriage (the last of these occurs early in the poem in *Tiruviruttam* 8 and 11, while the first two don't occur at all). Friedhelm Hardy charts the usage of the various Caṅkam tiṇais in the *Tiruviruttam*, and concludes that the mullai tiṇai (patient waiting/domestic happiness) dominates the mood of the poem, building on earlier Caṅkam associations of this landscape with Māyōṉ/Viṣṇu.[58]

The presence and place of Viṣṇu in the *Tiruviruttam* is, in a sense, straightforward. He is the poem's hero. It is no coincidence that Nammāḻvār refers to Viṣṇu in the poem's opening verse not by name or deed, but by addressing him in the vocative as *talaivā*: hero, leader. In Tamil poetic terms, he is both the *pāṭṭuṭai-t-talaivaṉ* (the hero of the poem) as well as the *kiḷavi-t-talaivaṉ* (hero of the narrative). As the pāṭṭuṭai-t-talaivaṉ he is a puṟam figure, cast as the patron ('listen to the petition', the *Tiruviruttam* begins), a somewhat removed recipient of the poem's praises and petitions. It is in this guise that Viṣṇu dominates the last fifteen verses, as the poet's voice increasingly becomes contiguous with the heroine's yearnings, demands and pleas for a direct, unmediated access to her king, her lord, her master.[59] A verse like this (*Tiruviruttam* 89) is typical of the tone in the poem's later section:

She Said:

Poison to evil fate sweetest nectar to virtue
beloved of the goddess whose seat is a lotus
strapping cowherd who grazed his cows
thinking nothing of it

that day measured worlds
with his two feet
bull-like lord my master
when will we be united?

Viṣṇu who measured the world, her bull-like lord, is also her/his master (*emmāṉ*), who can just as easily withhold or give grace. Throughout the *Tiruviruttam* he is pictured as a benevolent (puṟam) king whose just reign is threatened by his careless disregard for the poor girl's state—'your sceptre has bent this one time' the heroine, her friend and her mother all admonish on separate occasions.[60] Yet, not two verses earlier, in *Tiruviruttam* 87, Tirumāl is the heroine's longed-for beloved, for all intents the poem's kiḷavi-t-talaivaṉ. The heroine's mother laments:

The Mother Said:

In a heavy full-throated voice the a<u>nr</u>il laments.
In a loud voice waves crash into beautiful salt
marshes
hearing this
she praised the virtues of your brave bird

Now the world gossips
saying 'This is wrong'
O Tirumāl such is the fate of our precious girl.

We are in the world of the salt marshes, in the *neytal* tiṇai, the landscape of anxious, terrible waiting. The whole of the natural world—the monogamous *a<u>nr</u>il*s, the heartless waves—speak loudly of the girl's suffering joining the cacophony of cruel, heedless gossip. Is the girl of this verse contiguous with Nammāḻvār? The commentators answer in a vociferous affirmative. Is she the same speaker who in verse 89 quoted above refers to Viṣṇu as 'my master'?[61] Here too the commentators respond with an unequivocal agreement. Such doubling is not uncommon in the *Tiruviruttam*; it is in fact integral to creating experiential depth, an encounter echoed in many voices. It is no surprise then that the hero too is twinned, starring both as the poem's lover and the poem's patron. Only Tirumāl can end the girl's sorrow, because he is her lover (by uniting with her). Only Tirumāl can end Nammāḻvār's suffering because he is his king (by giving him grace). But such divisions are artificial, for the *Tiruviruttam* holds these multiple levels in perfect balance simultaneously. The poem is itself predicated on accepting that Nammāḻvār is the girl and himself, that Viṣṇu is both master and lover, that the action takes place in public with public demands for grace, and in private with private recollections of remembered union. In the *Tiruviruttam*, akam and puṟam, Nammāḻvār and his talaivi merge just as effectively as the pāṭṭuṭai-t-talaivaṉ and kiḷavi-t-talaivaṉ.[62]

In contrast—and this is one of the striking differences between the two poems—the *Tirukkōvaiyār* scrupulously keeps the pāṭṭuṭai-t-talaivaṉ and kiḷavi-t-talaivaṉ separate. Pērāciriyar, the celebrated thirteenth-century commentator on Tamil grammar and poetics, attended chiefly to the poem's erotic content, seeing it as a work high in literary achievement. But later Śaiva Siddhānta commentators reformulated his commentary to accommodate an allegorized theological meaning. As such, the poem's hero or kiḷavi-t-talaivaṉ becomes *uyir* (life/soul/breath), the heroine is Civam (Śiva) the supreme godhead, and the friend (tōḻi) is *aruḷ* (grace/mercy). Such allegoresis rests on conceiving the poem as existing simultaneously along two parallel tracks, identified as *ciṟṟiṉpam* (the lower love of human affections) and *pēriṉpam* (the higher love of spiritual desire).[63]

Awkward as such interpretations may be, they still enable the reader to make some sense of Śiva's absent presence in the *Tirukkōvaiyār*. As the poem's divine patron, Śiva is always present but remains outside and untouched by the *Tirukkōvaiyār*'s main action.[64] An exemplary case is *Tirukkōvaiyār* 71 spoken by the heroine's friend to comment on the lovers' union:

> Like the crow's two eyes
> that share a single pupil,
>   today these two share one life-breath
>   in separate bodies.

Here at the mountain of the lord
who combines all things in himself,
the lord who stays in Ambalam's great gardens,
this peacock of a woman and this man
share joy and pain alike.[65]

In this lovely verse that speaks of union, Śiva as the pāṭṭuṭai-t-talaivan̲ is invoked to grace the mountain-scape in much the same way that Viṣṇu as Māyōn̲ inhabits the mullai world. Here Śiva as mountain lord watches over the secret love of the anonymous heroine and her hero, the kiḷavi-t-talaivan̲. But Śiva does not participate in it. He provides the foundation on which such special love can grow; after all, he is the one 'who combines all things in himself'. He resides out there in the intimacy of the small hall, Tillai's Cir̲r̲ampalam, that most sacred of Inner Spaces. He is the heart of their love, nurtured into grace as it ripens between the hero and heroine. Such concentric embedding—Śiva out there but living inside the lovers who themselves are indivisible—is an unmistakable feature of the *Tirukkōvaiyār*. In David Shulman's fine distillation, such 'conflation or interpenetration of categories expresses a motivating tension between the overt eroticism of the poems and its extension or displacement into the divine realm'.[66] In the final sum, Śiva's poetic distance in the *Tirukkōvaiyār* expresses the very real, unbridgeable distance experienced by the poet from his beloved god.[67]

The *Tiruviruttam* and *Tirukkōvaiyār* purposefully set up an interlocking architecture that twins the outer world of mundane human love, the inner space of hidden desire, the people, personae, poets and gods that inhabit these spaces. So it is no surprise that in both poems the heroine is compared to sacred places—to sites like Tillai in the *Tirukkōvaiyār* and Vaikuṇṭha in the *Tiruviruttam*. Drawing again on the Caṅkam poetic tradition in which the lushness of a woman's beauty was oft compared to the prosperity of a great city (Toṇṭi, for instance), these two poems make such similes gesture towards the contiguity of the human and divine realms, of spaces shared by human beings and divinity alike.[68] If in the *Tirukkōvaiyār* the heroine is like Tillai, the most sacred of Śiva's terrestrial abodes, in the *Tiruviruttam* she is likened to Vaikuṇṭha, Viṣṇu's highest heaven. In the *Tiruviruttam*,

> She is equal to Vaikuṇṭha
> of the great lord who is fire water ether sky earth.
>
> *Tiruviruttam* 66

while in the *Tirukkōvaiyār* she is the

> Girl with the shining brow
> beautiful as Tillai,
> home of the lord
>   who vanquishes enemies . . .
>
> *Tirukkōvaiyār* 315[69]

And adroitly navigating the twin worlds of the human and the divine, what the Śrīvaiṣṇava commentators refer to as the *līlā vibhūti* (realm of play) and nitya vibhūti (eternal realm), is the human heart-mind (maṉam), that vast inner core of the poet, the inner space-place where god resides. Nammāḻvār is quick to make the point early on in the *Tiruviruttam*:

She Said:

Seeing
    the gentle woman dear to the flute-playing cowherd
Seeing
    goddess earth and Śrī
    inseparable as his shadow
will it remain there or return to me:

my lonely heart followed that bird
    of the king whose fiery disc
    scorches like his cool lovely tulasī
that bird praised by the gods
that bird whose anger burns like fire.

Tiruviruttam 3

while in the *Tirukkōvaiyār*, Māṇikkavācakar has this to say:

Did you go to study sweet Tamil verses
at the academy of Kūṭal,
high-walled city of the lord
    who dwells in my mind
    and in my heart,
    who stays at Tillai
    where flowing streams are held by dams.

Tirukkōvaiyār 20[70]

Both verses make the same point, albeit differently. In the *Tiruviruttam* the heart is unreliable, eternally abandoning the heroine to reside permanently with Viṣṇu. This of course depicts the situation perfectly, for she has in fact lost her heart to Viṣṇu. The movement towards union requires that the speaker follow the heart—it is externalized. In the *Tirukkōvaiyār*, the movement is inward. God is in Tillai, in Kūṭal, in *my* heart, in *my* mind.

Different as the *Tiruviruttam* and *Tirukkōvaiyār* may be, they are interpenetrating works, complements and mirrors of each other. Setting up dizzying involutions—heroine is the city of the lord who lives in her heart, a heart that periodically leaves her—the two poems constantly defeat the reader, disallowing simple concordances, forever deferring resolution. Margaret Trawick's observation in relation to the *Tirukkōvaiyār*—'the horizon is everywhere, including the place where we stand now'[71]—could just as easily describe the *Tiruviruttam*.

The Voices of Lament: Three Female Voices in the *Tiruviruttam*

Her Friend Said:

When that woman born from the lotus
her eyes cool as rain rose
from the white waves of the roaring dark sea
climbed on to his serpent bed

the maiden of the earth lamented loudly in the sky
her tears poured as rivers
flowing down her breasts, these mountains,
She cried 'Tirumāl is cruel.'

Tiruviruttam 52

The female voice dominates the *Tiruviruttam*. Speaking as heroine, friend, mother, fortune teller, this range of voices perceptively and insistently comments on the nature of a difficult, ill-fated love. In their strident voices, Nammāḻvār's women chastise, bemoan, curse, comfort, confide, weep, cry, console and lament. Their dramatic, striking speech deliberately draws attention to themselves and to their suffering: the mother loses her daughter to love; the daughter loses her heart to the absent god; the friend, a twin to the heroine, wastes away in sympathy. As the poem progresses, the female voices meld together, bound by the shared suffering of loss until they fully disappear by verse 88, absorbed, it would seem, into the singular voice of the speaker-poet. The appearance and disappearance of female voices is not peculiar to the *Tiruviruttam*. Āṇṭāḷ's *Nācciyār Tirumoḻi* uses the collective female voice of the *gopī*s of Āyarpāṭi to potent effect. They weave in and out of the poem at strategic moments until it becomes clear (particularly if you take the *Nācciyār Tirumoḻi* in concert with the *Tiruppāvai*) that union with Kṛṣṇa is to be found and savoured in the magical world of Vrindavan.[72] After all, in the *Nācciyār Tirumoḻi* Āṇṭāḷ leaves us at exactly the right place—in Vrindavan—to draw this conclusion. In the *Tiruvāymoḻi*, Nammāḻvār speaks in the female persona in approximately twenty-five decads, so a quarter of the text. The guise is so much a part of him that the Śrīvaiṣṇavas particularize it as the Parāṅkuśa Nāyikā. There are even elaborate *alaṅkāra*s (adornments) during the Annual Festival of Recitation in December when the image of Nammāḻvār is dressed as a woman or, more specifically, as the Parāṅkuśa Nāyikā. In such figurations, Nammāḻvār's heroine is not just an alter ego, another artificially forged self, but the truest voice of his deepest longing.

In typically self-reflexive fashion, the Śrīvaiṣṇava saṁpradāya has a long, rich history of trying to understand the purpose of the heroine/talaivi and her female companions in Nammāḻvār. The *Ācārya Hṛdayam* (The Heart of the Teacher), a thirteenth-century Maṇipravāḷa work, justifiably stands at the pinnacle of these engagements. Composed by Aḻakiya Maṇavāḷa Perumāḷ Nāyaṉār, a scion of the famous Vaṭakkuttiruvīti Piḷḷai, author of the authoritative *Īṭu* commentary on the *Tiruvāymoḻi*, the *Ācārya Hṛdayam* offers a succinct contemplation of Nammāḻvār's poetry and its philosophy in 234 *sūtra*s (referred to as *cūrṇikai*).[73] In many of these cūrṇikai, Nāyaṉār maps the development and use of the female voice.[74] The following famous cūrṇikai is typical of his style and his ability to distil the essence of generations of traditional thinking. In cūrṇikai 118, he says:

Jñāṉattil tam pēccu; prēmattil peṇ pēccu

In *jñāna* he speaks in his voice; in love, in a woman's voice.

In order to understand how Nāyaṉār comes to this point, we must place the cūrṇikai in context. Cūrṇikai 115 describes how union and separation nurture jñāna (wisdom, knowledge, discernment) and bhakti respectively. That is, jñāna indexes a state of *saṁśleṣa*, or union. Here, tight in the embrace of god who resides in one's own heart, he sees him in his mind's eye and thus enjoys him. Yet this is not a state that is sustained or, more accurately, cannot be sustained. Cūrṇikai 116 then offers the correlation between union and separation saying, '*ivaṟṟāl varum saṁśleṣa viśleṣaṅkaḷākiṟaṉa*' (what emerges from this is known as saṁśleṣa and *viśleṣa*). And soon, the āḻvār finds himself in a state of separation as though waking from a dream. It is in such a state, in viśleṣa—disengagement—that the female voice emerges. In cūrṇikai 119, the question is raised as to how words spoken in clarity (*teḷivu*) and in bewilderment (*kalakkam*), that is, in a state of saṁśleṣa and viśleṣa respectively, can be regarded as equally authoritative. Cūrṇikai 120 provides the definitive answer by asserting that whether he (Nammāḻvār) uses the masculine (*aṭiyōm*) or the feminine (*aṭicciyōm*), it is still his voice because his nature as a dependent (*pāratantriya*) remains unchanged. In the final analysis, it is the oscillations between saṁśleṣa and viśleṣa, between jñāna and bhakti that enable the cultivation of both wisdom and devotion.[75]

The *Ācārya Hṛdayam*'s sensitive understanding of the female voice is one way to approach the appearance and disappearance of female voices in the *Tiruviruttam*. In fact, everything that occurs in the poem after verse 87 indicates that full, immersive, abnegating union is the order of the day, a union that does not require the expressive, lamenting female voice. So, the speaker-poet can quite sensibly say that:

> When we see all that is like him
> when we see his emblems his form
> we stand entranced.
>
> *Tiruviruttam* 88

yet verses like this continue to intrude:

> Poison to evil fate sweetest nectar to virtue . . .
> bull-like lord my master
> when will we be united?
>
> *Tiruviruttam* 89

In the end, though, it would appear that the poised, philosophical voice wins in the *Tiruviruttam*; it concludes with the speaker-poet energetically exhorting fellow devotees to follow his lead as he 'awakens his desire' for Viṣṇu even as his helpless, confused female (and male) characters are left behind.

Although Nāyaṉār's lovely distillation provides us with one way of approaching the clamouring voices of the women in the *Tiruviruttam*, it opens up many more questions. Nāyaṉār and his fellow commentators are primarily concerned with *why* the female characters show up (answer: because of separation). There is little interest in *how* Nammāḻvār's female characters act and speak. What do they hope to achieve when they express a longing born of separation? Rather than see their words as emerging from the confusion and bewilderment (kalakkam) of painful separation, I propose that we read them as clear, thoughtful, passionate contemplations on the nature of such an experience. It is in the women's voices, more specifically in their *lamenting* voices, that the poem produces its willed, intentional ambiguities.

Laments mark separation, and generally that most final, inevitable of separations, death. Thick with vocatives, laments give expression to what Steven Hopkins has termed 'the vivid life of minute particulars'.[76] They enshrine a stubborn refusal to forget, to make the past matter in the present, and to draw attention to what (and who) is left behind.[77] It is no surprise then that lament songs in Tamil are called *oppu*, literally comparison, a means of cultivating a sympathetic understanding.[78] For example, here is a literary oppu from the great Tamil anthology of war poems, the *Puṟanāṉuṟu*. It is composed by King Pāri's daughters (1–3 CE) after he had fallen in battle. They say:

That day in that white moonlight
we had our father
enemies hadn't taken our hill.
This day in this white moonlight
kings with victory drums have taken our hill
and we have no father.

Puranānuru 112

This exquisite, hard-hitting verse encapsulates so much that is central to the Tamil lament. They are predicated on a feeling of lack, or *kurai*, that is itself built on an inadequacy, born from evaluation and comparison, of the living past in the frozen present.[79] So, we are back to oppu. Pāri's daughters had a father, now they have no father. They had a home, now they have no home. But implied in all of this is that someone else still has a father; someone else has a home—*their* home. In this frozen, unmoving moment of permanent, irreversible separation, it is the vivid particulars of the past that throb and tumble with life. Laments voice a stubborn refusal to forget just as clearly as they offer up unabashed critiques—of the present, of social order, of unjust rule, of oppressive hierarchies; and as women cry, weep and wail in real life or in poetry, their laments act as an ethical witness: their petition to be heard, their suffering to be acknowledged.[80]

Given that the *Tiruviruttam* styles itself as a viṇṇappam, a petition, it can be read as one long lament: a lament against this life of saṁsāra that thrives in the swamps of false knowledge and filthy bodies. It rails against the very injustice of a present life only made possible because of a morass of inescapable past deeds. The poem is as much a plea as it is a lament (*pulampal*), making this identification clearly in verse 86:

You who hold aloft disc and conch as weapons
stole butter then cried
when the cowherd woman bound you with ropes.
My lord what's left to say in my lament?[81]

The dissenting voices of the *Tiruviruttam*—all female—call attention to this desperate present life, petitioning Viṣṇu for his immediate intervention, to appear before her fully embodied, and most importantly to listen.[82] But in the *Tiruviruttam*'s universe the past is not all bad, for it marks the moments of union, fleeting though they may have been. As the heroine longs for reunion, the petition-lament takes on a different kind of urgency. In oppu, the female voices chorus

A past of blissful union telescopes into the miserable present: where is he?
She wastes away from lovesickness: where is he?
If even the geese and herons are united with their mates, why is she alone: where is he?

Such pointed questions and statements flow through the *Tiruviruttam* critiquing, shaming, eliciting sympathy: heroine, mother, friend all in oppu. Their tears flow freely, especially her tears, obscuring what she wants to see even as it sharpens the vision of the inner eye.[83] Conversely, she sees too much—the beauty of *his* eyes everywhere—and so too follows the despair. If she can see him, he must be outside of her, apart from her, separate. Our heroine can exult

Gleaming like a large lake of lotuses
on a dark vast mountain—
lord of this world bound by surging oceans

lord of the sky lord of the virtuous
that dark lord
my lord

I see the beauty of his eyes everywhere.

Tiruviruttam 39

Only to immediately lament to her beautifully adorned mothers that

the beautiful bull-like sun hides behind the mountain
dark night spreads everywhere
like a herd of elephants. . . .

O mothers, when will he glance at me?

Tiruviruttam 40

The vision is bifocal, turned both inwards and outwards, hearkening to the past and the present at once. The lament holds this bifocality in suspension as it urges towards dissolution, liquefaction. Her friend might say:

At this time in this city
the cool breeze abandons its nature
forgets everything breathes fire.
Is it to ruin the lustre of the girl
whose broad eyes spill tears like rain?

She weeps for cool lovely tulasī
from the one dark as rain clouds

whose sceptre has bowed
this one time.

Tiruviruttam 5

the mother might echo the sentiment:

The disease—its nature is deception—
makes her eyes broad as one's palm
seem like darting fish in a vast ocean.

Her heart is fixed on the honey-drenched tulasī
  of the one who lifted the mountain
  to protect his flock from the rain
  that one who rides the bird.
What will happen to her beautiful bangles now?

Tiruviruttam 24

and the heroine finds an echo, an oppu in the mournful evening:

Having lost the sun
the west wails cradling the moon at her waist
like a child, its mouth wet with milk
Such is the evening.

Those who love the tulasī
of the lord who measured worlds
have no relief
from the caress of the cold northern breeze.

Tiruviruttam 35

Oppu, comparison, sympathy are born from consonance, a consonance with others, with the landscape, between the past and the present. But sympathy, that precious virtue, is nurtured within a self that can dissolve, that is wet with emotion, with tears, what Tamils call the 'īramānā maṉam', the moist heart, the aqueous, acquiescent self: unbounded, fluid, malleable, ever flowing.[84] Is it any surprise then that the *Tiruviruttam* (as so many bhakti poems) is full of crying, where that *īram*—wetness—pours forth, unable to remain contained within the rigid contours of bodies? She cries, the clouds weep their tears as if in concert, and the cloud-hued lord is an absent presence. She cries a storm of tears, but that lord who lifted a mountain remains unmoved. He sends the breeze drenched with his *tulasī* instead: an absent presence. As tears, as clouds, as the honey dripping from tulasī, as milk staining the mouth of a suckling child, moistness leaks forth, bursting the banks of self and shores. It is the stuff of the lament, the stuff of oppu. As our heroine dissolves and disappears, nothing remains but water: she, melting and liquid, and god's own aqueous self:

These may be simple words. But this is the good I've seen
There is only the master of knowledge
that one who took the form of a boar
lifted the world submerged in crashing waves.

Neither for the gods
who possess the great tree of wishes
nor for all the others
is there anyone else.

Tiruviruttam 99

One Voice among Many: Revelation in the *Tiruviruttam*

Little worms that live in a wound
do what they do.
What do they know of the world?

I learned these songs from that cunning Tirumāl
who uses me to sing of himself.
It's like people making meaning
from the chirp of a lizard.

Tiruviruttam 48

Sandwiched between two verses of desperate longing, one spoken by the mother (*Tiruviruttam* 47) and one by the heroine (*Tiruviruttam* 49), appears this curious verse. The viṇṇappam which sets up the *Tiruviruttam* as an address to god has transmuted into an address *by* god. Nammāḻvār steps out of the frame, out of the female body to make space for the embodied presence of the deity. Correspondingly, the god enters the frame and embeds himself in the most inner of spaces, the devotee's heart-mind-self. In this centre of interiority, the space that enables an unconstructed expansion of self, the poet expands to become not just another thing, but an everything.[85] He is now an instrument, a vehicle, a *medium* through which god authors himself. For Hardy, this provides a rationale for the āḻvār's poetry that exists outside of himself, one made possible on account of the *Tiruviruttam*'s reliance on the symbolic structures of its Caṅkam-style characters, and which enable such instrumentality.[86]

The commentators of course have a differing perspective, and verses like this in the *Tiruviruttam* and *Tiruvāymoḻi* are what Francis Clooney has referred to as moments of god-identity or god-consciousness.[87] In the *Tiruvāymoḻi*, a striking instance of 'god-consciousness' is articulated in V.6, which follows a decad that describes the heroine's long, endless night of despair. In these ten verses the helpless mother tries to explain her daughter's strange claims—'I created Land and Sea'—to an invisible audience. The poet-heroine encompassed by god in turn encompasses the world, but it is an experience that remains inaccessible and opaque to everyone else.[88] God-identity in the *Tiruvāymoḻi* is not simply imitative, a persona that the heroine assumes like the gopīs of Vrindavan to alleviate suffering. Here her entire being is pervaded by god's presence in a self-obliterating possession.[89] Paradoxically, this ephemeral instance of god-consciousness occurs at the girl's nadir, when the anxieties of separation threaten to overwhelm her. Clooney's careful reading of the *Tiruvāymoḻi* commentators leads him to conclude accurately that separation activates such fierce concentration on the inner self that (s)he finds 'her true *ātman* within the *ātman*'.[90]

It is in a similar context that the *Tiruviruttam*'s first instance of god-consciousness makes itself known. The heroine's mother is concerned for her survival—can she survive another night, another onslaught of the breeze? Can she live in this terrible world? This is the stage that the poet sets for us in the *Tiruviruttam* and one that Periyavāccāṉ Piḷḷai deftly directs us through. He tells us that as Nammāḻvār grieves for a pointless life on this terrestrial realm, Viṣṇu responds that it is to sing of him as he would in Vaikuṇṭha that he lives here in the world of play, the līlā vibhūti. To prove this very point, cunning, playful Viṣṇu takes Nammāḻvār over (*visayīkarittu*) to sing and enjoy his own form (*svarūpa-rūpa*), his virtues (*guṇa*) and his *vibhūti*s (realms). As we have already seen, such moments of intermittent takeover are not unusual in Nammāḻvār (or in bhakti poetry in general). Despite the situational similarity between V.6 and *Tiruviruttam* 47–48, Periyavāccāṉ Piḷḷai does not direct us to a decad like V.6 to explore this particular instance of god-consciousness. Instead, he provides us with an apt parallel from *Tiruvāymoḻi* VII.9, a decad in which Nammāḻvār speaks again of Viṣṇu singing of himself through the poet. From this rich ten verses full of textured descriptions of Viṣṇu's uncompromising takeover, Piḷḷai chooses to cite a single phrase: *eṉ muṉ collum*, he who sings in front of me, from VII.9.2. Let us see this verse in its entirety:

> What can I say? Now becoming one with my sweet life,
> he makes me sing sweet songs with my own words
> with his own words the lord of illusion praises himself,
> **the one who sings before me**, the first of the three forms.[91]

With this citation Piḷḷai subtly brings us back to the petition that begins the *Tiruviruttam*—stand before me embodied—and the poet is now not so much taken over by Viṣṇu as directed by him, reduced to striving to make meaning of what he is taught. He is rendered speechless: 'What can I say?' *Tiruvāymoḻi* VII.9.2 begins.[92] All of this echoes in the only other god-consciousness verse that occurs late in the *Tiruviruttam*.

> Virtuous Vedic seers
> are blessed to be adorned by
> your dark body your red lotus eyes your feet.

Like a blind cow mimicking the lowing herd
so it can return to the city
I repeat some words.
What else can this servant say?

Tiruviruttam 94

Here is the poet once again in a kind of self-defeating moment. His experience consigned to mimicry, undertaken with neither knowledge nor understanding, it is set against the grand ritual actions of the seers and sages. Certainly, the poet-speaker is well prepared for simple imitation, having practised mindlessly repeating the god's names and places like a mad thing (*Tiruviruttam* 20, 60, 71, 83). Having set such a precedent, without quite saying it, he tells us that it is better to be a blind cow than a vaunted sage, it is better to repeat *his* names and deeds, than lofty Vedic chants. Even if his final words are simple, low, base (the deprecating *īṉaccol* that begins the very important ninety-ninth verse), they emerge from Nammāḻvār's direct apprehension. This is the good (*nallatu*) the poet has seen: there is no one but the master of knowledge, *jñāna-p-pirāṉ allāl illai*. He is all things and all words, words both low and high. He speaks these words, but, equally, they are spoken to him. He stands embodied to listen—we are back where we started—and then, trickster that he is, embodies himself within the devotee to speak of *him*.

So now to the poem's cast of characters we add Viṣṇu himself. As the frame shatters and the petition transforms into lamentation into revelation we are left wondering: who speaks? One answer would be that *he* speaks through Nammāḻvār who multiplies his self to speak in his many voices, in his many personae. Immersed in each other, the poet and his deity speak in boisterous multivocality, their many selves porous and permeable to each other. Writing in the context of Sanskrit drama, David Shulman points out that the self expands through disintegration, splitting, viśleṣa. In that state of disengagement the self sees itself as though from a distance (self-reflexivity?), mirroring and doubling itself.[93] In the *Tiruviruttam*, the heroine becomes Nammāḻvār's double, and she becomes his mirror. The friend becomes her reflection, the means for the heroine to make sense of the oscillations of desire. The hero and heroine twin each other, a perfectly matched love-struck pair. And Viṣṇu doubles as both hero and patron. Finally, in the moment of possession (god-consciousness), as the boundaries of this polyphonic self are breached, poet and god quite literally become mirrors of the other, the poet content to simply and uncomprehendingly repeat the words he is taught. Immersed as he is in god (an āḻvār, after all!), such mirroring enables him to continue to have a relationship with his beloved lord. The vast 'horizons of encompassment'[94] that such possession makes possible permit the god to remain simultaneously inside our poet and outside him, for the poem to thus be petition, lamentation and revelation.

But there is more to possession in the *Tiruviruttam*. In both *Tiruviruttam* 48 and 94, the poet's (god's?) words function like a *kuṟi*, a sign or mark, and, more generally, divination. The poet himself draws attention to the kuṟi-like function of the *Tiruviruttam* by comparing his feeble poetic attempts to making meaning out of the chirp of a lizard, a common means of divination in Tamil Nadu (*Tiruviruttam* 48).[95] Often the telling of kuṟi occurs through possession, when the deity descends to speak through an agent to resolve illness and conflicts. In Caṅkam poems the disease is lovesickness, a diagnosis the diviner misses without fail. Nammāḻvār too exploits this trope to full effect as in *Tiruviruttam* 20, while turning it on its head.

The Friend Said:

The great god causes this quiet girl's disease
It's not the disease of the young god
who demands things to end it.

O Vēlaṉ, stop now.
Mother, listen to me
Repeat the names of the one who swallowed the
seven worlds
adorn her with his garland of lovely cool tulasī.

The friend counsels the mother that this is no disease of possession (at least not the possession of Murukaṉ), and is instead lovesickness for Māl. But is this *just* lovesickness? Is there not something of possession here, marked by its attendant loss of consciousness and its merging of distinct selves? The fortune teller seems to understand this and in her lone verse responds obliquely:

This girl whose breasts are covered by cloth
has the divine disease
inflicted by the virtue
of the master of the gods.

Bring a garland of divine cool lovely tulasī
or even its leaves its stalk its roots

or just earth on which it grows
place it on her.

Tiruviruttam 53

Soon thereafter, the heroine herself confirms the true nature of this divine disease (*taiva nal nōy*) which so consumes her:

Beautiful friend don't be afraid
we survived because of the grace
of the lord who swallowed this wide world

a breeze cool as a rain cloud
came bearing the sweet fragrance of lovely tulasī
it caressed my senses my jewels
but no one else knows.

Tiruviruttam 56

Both *Tiruviruttam* 20 and 56, verses about the 'divine disease', share the same skilful use of the myth of Viṣṇu swallowing/eating the worlds to suggest the intimate relationship between the poet and god, between the heroine and her divine beloved. John Carman and Vasudha Narayanan identify the swallowing of the world as a root metaphor in the *Tiruvāymoḻi*, which Nammāḻvār cleverly associates with union with god.[96] Erotically charged, the myth evokes the god and devotee's mutually voracious appetite for each other. It links to other similarly charged divine gustatory indulgences—the churning of the ocean to yield its nectar, the stealing of the butter. All of these myths are present in the *Tiruviruttam*. They never appear together, although these three myths are often clustered, suggesting that we are meant to apprehend the implied relationships.[97] Eating butter is to eating nectar is to eating the world is to eating the deity. Is it any wonder then that everything seems to be ravenous in the *Tiruviruttam*? Night devours the day; the moon suckles like a child. The breeze eats the honey-drenched tulasī, the tulasī eats its own honey, and it is this nectar-filled tulasī that is the sole cure for the heroine's illness. She hungers for union, and without it she starves. She empties out and her bangles slip off. The only thing that can fill her is *his* presence. In all of its iterations, eating and swallowing (and its inverse, spitting out) invoke not just union but complete pervasion, the 'horizons of encompassment'.[98] Even when speaking in negatives, the implications are clear: once swallowed, he is all things to her, dark fruit, the sea and even the end of days:

> I didn't say 'He became the end of days and
> swallowed the seven worlds.'
> I saw a dark fruit
> observed 'It's the colour of the sea.'
>
> My mother then said 'What impertinence!'
> 'She speaks of the colour of the one who swallowed
> worlds.'
> Speak to her dear friend. My mother scolds me.
>
> *Tiruviruttam* 71

Bodies of Enjoyment: The *Tiruviruttam* and Commentary

Śrīvaiṣṇava commentators, beginning with Periyavāccāṉ Piḷḷai (thirteenth century), recognize two levels of meaning in the *Tiruviruttam*. The outer level is the anyāpadeśa (the other meaning) and the svāpadeśa (esoteric meaning) is its secret, inner meaning. In Tamil terms, such ingenious splicing finds expression in the terms ciṟṟiṉpam (lower or minor love) and pēriṉpam (higher or major love), concepts that guide the interpretation of poems like the *Tirukkōvaiyār*. In the Śrīvaiṣṇava context, the allegoresis required to divide and merge a text is refined throughout the long, dense (continuing) history of commentarial activity. The definitive *Ācārya Hṛdayam* (thirteenth century), primarily concerned with Nammāḻvār's *Tiruvāymoḻi*, synthesizes prevailing interpretive modes, and provides the tools to decode the anyāpadeśa, allowing one to peer into the poet's heart as though through clear glass, in an active reading process that Francis Clooney has rightly termed 'seeing through texts'.[99]

A fundamental guiding principle of Śrīvaiṣṇava commentary is the notion of *anubhava* (enjoyment). Commentary is not meant simply to elucidate and decode; rather, it is meant to induce, mimic and replicate divine savouring. In other words, commentary too is guided by aesthetic concerns and seeks to produce an aesthetic affect. Within this paradigm, Śrīvaiṣṇava commentary is conceived of as an *anubhava grantha*, a text of enjoyment, a term that understands pleasure (expressed as anubhava) as central to their theological project. Conceptualized as such, a proper commentary succeeds only when it acts as an effective and affective conduit between the āḻvār's savouring of god and the reader/listener. Just as the āḻvār is a vessel filled to brimming with god's presence, to produce a flavourful commentary the āḻvār's experience must inhabit the commentator. Such exegesis becomes a delicately balanced, multi-tiered edifice of enjoyment, recording both the mutual relish of Viṣṇu and the āḻvār's savouring of god and the commentator's own savouring of both. So how does the Śrīvaiṣṇava commentator go about generating anubhava both within himself and in his audience? How does a commentary proceed? What are the sources he turns to?

While several āḻvār poems are inspired by Caṅkam (akam) verses—the *Tiruviruttam* is a case in point—Śrīvaiṣṇava commentators rarely reference or cite them. Often this disregard of the earlier largely secular Tamil sources has been taken as evidence of either the commentator's ignorance or of the fading relevance and circulation of the great Caṅkam works.[100] Glancing at the references in the commentaries to poems like the *Tiruviruttam* amply demonstrates that the Śrīvaiṣṇava commentators were well aware of the literary past, but that they simply chose not to turn to it for their exegetical purposes. Instead, they adroitly employ *both* Tamil and Sanskrit sources to elucidate āḻvār poetry to fulfil newly emergent theological and aesthetic imperatives. While the Sanskrit sources are far-ranging—the Upaniṣads, Purāṇas and the epics loom large—āḻvār poetry provides the bulk of their Tamil sources. As all these texts—Sanskrit and Tamil—are seen to embody that elusive quality of anubhava, they are regarded as specifically suited to heightening one's own experience of the āḻvār poem. Let us leave aside the Sanskrit corpus for a moment and examine why Śrīvaiṣṇava commentators privilege āḻvār poetry over the citation of relevant Tamil literary sources.[101] Most obviously, to the commentator a line from the *Tiruvāymoḻi* or one from Tirumaṅkai's *Periya Tirumoḻi* captures accurately the peculiar oscillations of mystical experience in a way that the archetypal love poems of the Caṅkam anthologies simply cannot. Each āḻvār becomes a light to another; one anubhava telescopes into another; the *Tiruvāymoḻi* weaves into the *Tiruviruttam*; Nammāḻvār transforms into Tirumaṅkai, into Parāṅkuśa Nāyikā, into Āṇṭāḷ. In the end, anubhava is produced through a glorious intermingling and a heady intertextuality where all āḻvār poems are seen as commentaries and elucidations on each other.[102]

A.K. Ramanujan in *Hymns for the Drowning* theorizes the relationship between Viṣṇu and Nammāḻvār in the *Tiruvāymoḻi* in terms of mutual cannibalism, where 'the eater is eaten, the container is contained in a metonymy many times over'.[103] The *Tiruviruttam* too is replete with mutual devouring, such that the boundaries between Nammāḻvār, his many multiplying selves (heroine, friend, mother, self, etc.) and Viṣṇu are not just breached, but dissolved. So many times in the *Tiruviruttam* we are at a loss to determine *who* the speaker might be, with the knowledge that Nammāḻvār stands behind them all, and that behind him stands Viṣṇu, both listening and speaking. In writing about the *Tirukkōvaiyār*, in many ways the *Tiruviruttam*'s fraternal twin, David Shulman characterizes such involution as mutual embeddedness, a strategy designed to confound speaker(s) and listener(s) as they push inexorably towards dissolution.[104] One can make similar comparisons of mutual cannibalism/mutual embeddedness when we consider what Śrīvaiṣṇava commentary seeks to do. If anubhava is a central goal of commentary, it can only be sufficiently realized by breaking the artificial divides between poet and commentator, poem and commentary. When the commentator calls up the various āḻvār and their respective poems to elucidate the work of another, it serves to highlight that they speak in many voices, through many selves of a singular experience. This is not to say that the Śrīvaiṣṇava commentator is indifferent to difference and nuance; rather, the commentary seeks threads of commonality, of echo, of mutual embeddedness where each poet feeds off the other while nonetheless remaining distinct. One might consider here how this notion of embeddedness in commentary finds exemplary expression in the famous story of the meeting of the first three āḻvār. Poykai, Pēy and Pūtam encounter each other in a rainstorm when they take shelter in a temple. Once inside, they are pushed, then crushed together by Viṣṇu's encompassing presence. The boundary of each—they are already fluid and disembodied—dissolves into the other, and then into Viṣṇu.[105] In the end, their mutual experience of simultaneous fullness and emptiness results in three similar poems.[106]

In Poykai's words:

Taking the earth as bowl,
the vast sea as oil,
and the burning sun as my lamp,
I laid this garland of verses
at the feet of the lord
who holds a dazzling red wheel

to keep the ocean of sorrows far away.

Mutal Tiruvantāti 1[107]

Pūtam's take:

With love as bowl,
ardor as oil,
and a joyful mind as wick,
I swooned
and lit a blazing lamp of knowledge
for Nāraṇaṉ,

even as I delight in the sage Tamil tongue.

Iraṇṭām Tiruvantāti 1[108]

and Pēy's exults:

I lit the lamp of discernment,
I searched for the lord,
and caught him in my net—
then the lord of illusions quietly entered my heart
and there
he stands, sits, and reclines
always without flaw.

Mūṉṟām Tiruvantāti 94[109]

While Poykai, Pēy and Pūtam may be an obvious example of how mutual embeddedness/cannibalism might work, a Śrīvaiṣṇava commentary is guided by philosophical *and* aesthetic obligations to identify, construct and cultivate such moments. It is through this process that anubhava occurs.[110]

Let us now return to the *Tiruviruttam* and Periyavāccāṉ Piḷḷai's commentary to examine how a skilled commentator might seek to nurture anubhava in himself and in his audience. The poem has its inbuilt audience—the mother, the friend, the hero and even the natural world—who engage in a kind of sympathetic anubhava of the heroine's angst. In the svāpadeśa, the poem's supporting cast members are Nammāḻvār's devotees—bhāgavatas—who comfort him through the ebb and flow of his longing. Their love for Nammāḻvār reverberates in the love he has for Viṣṇu. Through this vicarious, resonant relish anubhava is born, and it is nurtured into voracious savouring through the productive symbiosis between the poem's two registers.

Nammāḻvār himself signals the *Tiruviruttam*'s two interpenetrating frames by characterizing the poem as a viṇṇappam. Thus bracketed, the love poem (*akapporuḷ*) quite literally becomes akam (inner), enclosed in the embrace of the poem's first verse and its final verse, the phala śruti. Yet this inner poem is also just the outer meaning: it is puṟam. The hidden inner (akam) meaning is secreted into these akam verses of the mundane puṟam world, embedded as god is embedded in Nammāḻvār, as Nammāḻvār is embedded within god. The task of the commentator is to draw together seamlessly the *Tiruviruttam*'s implicit meaning in the poem's inner verses. In doing so, the poem's inner meaning becomes public (after all, that's the purpose of commentary), while the external shell is interred. To put it simply, akam is to svāpadeśa as puṟam is to anyāpadeśa, even as the akapporuḷ verses of the *Tiruviruttam* look to Caṅkam akam poetry for inspiration. To further extend the metaphor of akam and puṟam, the commentary becomes the poem's public face mediating its inner worlds. But in the dance of akam and puṟam, whether within the *Tiruviruttam* or in how we approach Śrīvaiṣṇava commentary in general, they are not antagonists set against each other. They are complementary, fitting together as a jigsaw, each nestled into the other as svāpadeśa and anyāpadeśa, as poem and commentary.

There are several important commentaries to the *Tiruviruttam* as befits Nammāḻvār's status as the pre-eminent āḻvār, but are far fewer than those composed for his *Tiruvāymoḻi*. Below I discuss the *Tiruviruttam* commentary authored by Periyavāccāṉ Piḷḷai (b. 1128), the student of the formidable scholar Nampiḷḷai, and offer an example of Periyavāccāṉ Piḷḷai's commentary to a *Tiruviruttam* verse. I have chosen to focus on Periyavāccāṉ Piḷḷai for several reasons. He is the only medieval commentator to compose commentaries on the entire *Nālāyira Divya Prabandham*, earning him the title *vyākhyāna cakravarti* (emperor of commentators). His writing also represents the maturation of Śrīvaiṣṇava Maṇipravāḷa prose discourse, and in many places (in his work on the *Tiruviruttam* and elsewhere) anticipates the internal philosophical differences that eventually lead several centuries later to a sectarian split. Finally, Piḷḷai's commentarial voice is lively and energetic. His love for the *Vālmīki Rāmāyaṇa* expresses itself through an abundance of allusions to and citations from that text, while he demonstrates his erudition by also quoting liberally from Sanskrit scriptural sources. All of this sits comfortably beside references from the works of the āḻvār and contemporary anecdotal evidence. Piḷḷai's commentarial style is thorough and rigorous. In his *Tiruviruttam* commentary he takes care to elucidate the anyāpadeśa meaning by identifying the specific poetic situations, with colophonic statements such as 'the friend comforts the heroine when the rains arrive'.[111] He also attempts to establish narrative continuities within the text wherever possible. His commentary, composed in a dialogic style, is imaginative and thick with allusions. It also follows fairly closely the well-established contours that owe as much to literary commentators like Uraiyāciriyar as to philosophers and theologians writing in Sanskrit and Tamil.

Periyavāccāṉ Piḷḷai's Maṇipravāḷa commentary for the *Tiruviruttam* consists of three major parts:[112]

1. **A Word-Gloss**: In some instances this is the first level of interpretation. The gloss itself consists of two parts—where the commentator reorders the words of the poem into prose order and these reordered phrases/words are interrupted by the actual gloss. In *Tiruviruttam* 1 the word *tēvar* (literally, gods) occurs. Piḷḷai, in accordance with preceding commentarial practice and Śrīvaiṣṇava philosophy, glosses it as *nityasūri* (eternal/perfect beings) referring to those who dwell with Viṣṇu permanently. Ādi Śeṣa, Garuḍa and Viśvaksena may be said to be the foremost among the nityasūris.
2. **A Context and Continuity (*Saṅgati*)**: Here the commentator establishes continuity with a previous verse. In a poem like the *Tiruviruttam* this continuity has to be established along the two parallel lines of anyāpadeśa and svāpadeśa. The section also sometimes provides a brief synopsis of the verse.
3. **The Commentary Proper**: Here the commentator explicates each phrase (following the word order established in the gloss) and creates a sustained interpretation of the verse. The commentary is characterized by frequent quotations from the poems of the āḻvār, and Sanskrit sources such as the Bhagavad Gītā, the *Vālmīki Rāmāyaṇa* and the *Viṣṇu Purāṇa*. The commentator also often uses anecdotes from the lives of significant historical figures like Rāmānuja and Kūrattāḻvāṉ to elucidate the veracity of

his claims. These anecdotes take several forms—a retelling of a story involving their experience of āḻvār poetry; an interpretation of a line of āḻvār poetry which is cast as a dialogue between them and a student; the quotation of a line attributed to a figure like Rāmānuja. The length of the commentary depends on the significance of individual verses to the commentator's interpretative agenda.

Despite the rigorous demands of commentarial structure, Periyavāccāṉ Piḷḷai is no stuffy pedant. He is attuned to nuance and to the *Tiruviruttam*'s ever-shifting centres. He is attentive to how the poem continually displaces meaning through willed ambiguity, which manifests through a confusion of speaking voices or through multiple possible readings of a given verse effected by the manipulation of antāti or other kinds of wordplay. *Tiruviruttam* 25 is a good example of both elements and typical of Piḷḷai's approach.

eṅkōl vaḷai mutalā kaṇṇaṉ maṇṇum viṇṇum aḷikkum
ceṅkōl vaḷaivu viḷaivikkumāl tiṟal cēr amarar
tam kōṉuṭaiya tam kōṉ umpar ellā evarkkum tamkōṉ
nam kōṉ ukakkum tuḻāy eṉ ceyyātu iṉi nānilattē

She Said:

If my beautiful bangles make Kaṇṇaṉ's sceptre
which rules earth and sky
bend

what will it not do—that tulasī
dear to the king of valiant gods,
king of the heavens,
our king?

Piḷḷai begins by suggesting that the above verse may be spoken by either the heroine or her friend, reading the verse's opening phrase, *eṅkōl vaḷai*, as 'my beautiful bangles' (heroine) or as an epithet, 'she who wears beautiful bangles' (heroine's friend). In the commentary for this same verse, attentive to its grammar, Piḷḷai also suggests that it can be read either by taking Kaṇṇaṉ or *tuḻāy* (tulasī) as the subject. In the former case, the entire verse is read as a single sentence, while in the second case the *āl* in the second line (*viḷaivikkumāl*) is taken as an exclamation of surprise. In this interpretation, the verse splits into two parts.[113] For simplicity and to convey how differently the verse reads in the alternative proposition, I have removed all the epithets and reduced the two parts of this latter reading to two straightforward prose sentences:

> Kaṇṇaṉ's sceptre, which rules earth and sky, bent because of my bangles.
> What won't the tulasī of my lord do now?

Keeping all this in mind—the complementary relationships between commentary and text, the mutual embeddedness of anyāpadeśa and svāpadeśa, the imaginative and sensitive readings that Piḷḷai offers—let us turn to Piḷḷai's full-length commentary on a single verse of the *Tiruviruttam*.[114] I have chosen verse 68, one with clear akapporuḷ content from the poem's latter half. It is also a verse translated and discussed by A.K. Ramanujan to draw parallels between the Caṅkam literary tradition and the poetry of Nammāḻvār, a similarity that Piḷḷai barely mentions in his commentary.[115] Piḷḷai's commentarial style is difficult to translate, so what appears below is a paraphrase of the main part of the commentarial text.[116] First the verse in Tamil and then in translation:

malarntē oḻintila mālaiyum mālai-p-poṉ vācikaiyum
pulam tōy taḻai-p-pantal taṇṭu uṟa nāṟṟi-p-porukaṭal cūḻ
nilam tāviya em perumāṉ taṉatu vaikuntam aṉṉāy
kalantār varavu etir koṇṭu vaṉ koṉṟaikaḷ kārttaṉavē

Her Friend Said:

O girl like Vaikuṇṭha
of the great lord
who spanned this world surrounded by swirling oceans
the lovely koṉṟai begin to bud
awaiting your lover's return

they haven't yet bloomed
into dense garlands of gold
that hang from a thick canopy of leaves.

The Situational Context

This verse falls into a category known in Caṅkam poetics as *kālamayakkam* (the mixing up of seasons). Although Piḷḷai doesn't actually use the phrase, it is clear from his exposition that he is well aware of the specific poetic situation that Nammāḻvār's verse describes. After union the heroine (talaivi) is separated from her lover (talaivaṉ), who had promised to return by the time the *koṉṟai* bloomed, a mark of the rainy season. That time has arrived, those flowers have blossomed, but he is yet to return. The heroine, observing these signs, is depressed. Witnessing her suffering, the heroine's friend (tōḻi) assures her that it is not 'that' time yet. Although the buds of the koṉṟai may have appeared—she cannot deny the direct evidence before her—there is still time for his return, for the buds are yet to bloom.

Anyāpadeśa

The commentary is composed as an imagined dialogue between the talaivi and tōḻi. It begins with the exposition of the verse's key opening phrase, *malarntē oḻintila* (they have not bloomed). The heroine queries, 'How can you say that they haven't bloomed? The time has come when they are blooming everywhere.' The friend responds, 'Indeed, but they have not yet bloomed; only their buds have appeared.'

In the verse, the flowers are described as *pulam-tōy*, which Periyavāccāṉ Piḷḷai interprets as 'touching the earth' in his initial word-gloss, but in the thick of the commentary, he expands the phrase to encompass three further readings. First, taking *pulam* as 'senses', he offers that the flowers are so beautiful that they entrance the senses. Next, returning to the original gloss he explains that the koṉṟai tree branches touch the ground because they are weighted down by their blossoming flowers. In the final instance, he interprets the entire phrase—*pulam tōy taḻai-p-pantal taṇṭu uṟa nāṟṟi* (hanging from the canopy of leaves / to touch the ground)—in an evocative and imaginative manner, seeing the dense covering of leaves as the tree's [thousand] eyes. The implication here is that the entire natural world is alive and a witness to the heroine's unbearable suffering. It is in such moments, subtle and easily missed, that the commentary achieves texture, building anubhava. While Piḷḷai doesn't reference the Caṅkam poem that Nammāḻvār's verse is modelled on (*Kuṟuntokai* 66), his interpretation for just this one line of verse indicates that he is well aware of the norms of Caṅkam poetics, where so often the characters' bodies and their feelings—untamed and untameable as the natural world—are contiguous with the natural world that they inhabit.[117]

For Piḷḷai, the most significant moment of the poem is the comparison of the heroine (talaivi) to Vaikuṇṭha (*vaikuntam annāy*). It is in the exposition of this phrase that Piḷḷai really hits his stride. Likening the talaivi to Vaikuṇṭha, Viṣṇu's eternal realm (nitya vibhūti), implies that she too cannot be destroyed. The friend asks rhetorically, 'Will he [Viṣṇu] allow you to be destroyed?' But even if she were equated to the impermanent terrestrial plane (līlā vibhūti), which is subject to the cycles of creation and dissolution, he would protect her and prevent her destruction. After all, did he not span the earth and through this action shelter it? The tōḻi proceeds to say that if the talaivi continues to despair, it only demonstrates that she is unaware of her own worth (that she is like Vaikuṇṭha) and of his form and his nature (*svarūpa/svabhāva*). It is in his nature to unite with her as Viṣṇu too cannot be separated for long from those he loves. After all, did he not come to her once before?

Then, returning to the central image of the poem—the flowering trees—Piḷḷai (in the voice of the friend) goes on to assert that when even non-sentient beings (*acetana*) like the trees know to wait for Viṣṇu, how can one like her (implying that she is special) quail in misery in this fashion? The koṉṟai are strong, for they are certain that he will come as promised. They are steadfast in their patient waiting for his arrival. In fact, they are not waiting for the rain, but for him.

Once again, we have here an instance of Piḷḷai's wonderfully suggestive, oblique commentarial style. In the natural world, the koṉṟai's buds appear anticipating the rain clouds. But Piḷḷai overturns this by denying that the flowers are awaiting the rains; instead, they too are waiting for Viṣṇu. In this, their waiting is akin to that of the heroine. But it cannot escape even the most casual reader that Viṣṇu's cool, dark body *is* the body of the rain clouds and vice versa. In Piḷḷai's masterful framing of this interpretation, both tree and heroine await the arrival of their beloved, who brings relief/grace that is cool. Again, while there is no evocation of the proper tiṇai in Piḷḷai's commentary, the idea of steadfast, patient waiting that characterizes the mullai tiṇai—set in the time of rains and signalling domestic happiness—is invoked in the friend's quiet admonishment and also her assurance that the heroine will be reunited with her beloved.[118]

Svāpadeśa

Piḷḷai's svāpadeśa for this verse is short and to the point. The verse celebrates him (Viṣṇu) who because of his virtues and in his wisdom (*guṇa-jñāṉam*) protects Vaikuṇṭha (nitya vibhūti) and the earth (līlā vibhūti) after first destroying the latter. In this manner, the bhāgavatas (disciples/devotees) comforted Nammāḻvār when the rains arrived.

Although the svāpadeśa for this verse is brief, it ably demonstrates how Piḷḷai establishes continuities between svāpadeśa and anyāpadeśa, while setting individual readings in the context of his meta-interpretation. The concordance here of bhāgavata = friend and Nammāḻvār = heroine remains consistent with the equivalences established in the poem's opening verses. The argument that the *Tiruviruttam* celebrates Viṣṇu's virtues and his wisdom—a point of significance, because the poem ends by declaring that there is no one but the jñāna-p-piraṉ (master of wisdom)—iterates the anyāpadeśa's central thesis. The heroine is like Vaikuṇṭha and he will protect her for that is his nature, again an argument made repeatedly and forcefully in the *Tiruviruttam*, which in its final word identifies jñāna-p-pirā<u>n</u> with Varāha, Viṣṇu in his avatāra as the boar (*Tiruviruttam* 99).

Nonetheless, whether Viṣṇu rescued the earth or ate it up, whether he measured it or protected it, it is also his nature to destroy this līlā vibhūti, the world of saṁsāra, only to renew it again. The larger theological point of course, which Piḷḷai only suggests above but which the poem takes pains to record, is that the talaivi's/Nammāḻvār's gradual destruction, dissolution, erasure is necessary to finally make way for a new self fully awakened to Viṣṇu's eternal presence within her and in all things. Viewed through this lens, all the instances of repetition and mimicry (whether in the context of revelation or madness—perhaps they are the same?) function as interpretive moments. The girl repeats the names of god as she has been taught. This is madness in her mother's judgement. We (and the poet) know better. The poet comments on his own experience: I repeat what Māl tells me to, interpreting it as arbitrarily (or so he claims) as the chirp of a lizard. Viṣṇu enjoys the poem as its audience and as its author, and is himself enjoyed by the poet. In the end, the poet cheekily informs us that his (god's?) words are base and simple. But they say profound things if you know how to read and how to experience the tale. In a typical snake-eating-its-tail involution, the poem becomes a commentary on itself, its own anubhava grantha.

Prior Elopements: The *Tiruviruttam* in English Translation

A Hundred Measures of Time follows a modest clutch of English-language translations of the *Tiruviruttam*. I survey and discuss below the most significant of these efforts. My primary concern here is not to evaluate the quality of the translations—many suffer the curse of turgid Indologese, that peculiar Victorian-inflected register that has plagued English-language translations of Indian works—but rather to explore the specific historical moments that produced them. The *Tiruviruttam*'s difficulty and obscurity has not diminished its appeal, and each of the translations discussed below have sought to find their own way through the thick density of Nammāḻvār's poetic universe.

The first effort was undertaken by J.S.M. Hooper (1882–1974), a British Wesleyan Methodist minister who was based in Madras and Nagpur.[119] The *Tiruviruttam* is the last entry in his 1929 anthology *Hymns of the Ālvārs*. The work was commissioned by J.N. Farquhar (1861–1929) for The Heritage of India Series, which was meant to popularize the regional literary and devotional literatures of India.[120] In a private prospectus written in either 1913 or 1914, Farquhar affirmed that The Heritage of India Series must seek out and showcase the best of India so that it may be 'known, enjoyed and used' while not shying away from what is perceived of as unhealthy.[121] These ideas are reinforced in the Editorial Preface to the *Hymns of the Tamil Śaivite Saints* (1921) in which the reader is assured that all the books in the series are vetted for their keen scholarship and deep sympathy.[122] The Heritage of India series was seen as fulfilling a need, chiefly by offering an alternative to the expensive, technical, scholarly tomes that were already in circulation; an affordable counterpart that would allow every educated Indian access to the treasures of his past.[123] As of 1921, Farquhar had already co-edited with Bishop Vedanayagam Samuel Azariah (1874–1945) a bilingual translation of the Tamil Śaiva poets—*Hymns of the Tamil Śaivite Saints*—for the same series, this one a collaboration between two translators from the United Theological College, Bangalore: Francis Kingsbury and Godfrey E. Phillips (1878–1961).[124] Phillips, a member of the London Missionary Society (LMS) and a professor at the United Theological College (founded in 1910 in a joint effort by the LMS and the Wesleyan Methodist Missionary Society), had also been active in seeking cooperation between the various missions.[125]

As principal of Wesley College, Madras, and steeped in Church-related activity in south India, Hooper was the ideal candidate to undertake the āḻvār translation effort. He fit Farquhar's stringent standards to have missionaries and Indian Christians produce 'scholarly work that can be trusted, to use the experience they have of the people in interpreting the religions of India'[126] while adhering to the three key principles of 'a. accuracy, b. sympathy and c. uncompromising faithfulness to Christ'.[127] In addition, Hooper was active in promoting Christian literature, a project dear to Farquhar through his service on the General Committee of the Indian Literature Fund.[128] Although Farquhar claims to have wanted to encourage Indian Christians to participate in his three major publishing endeavours (The Indian Religious Life Series, The Heritage of India Series and The Quest of India Series), the evidence points to the contrary. By the time he left India in 1923, there was only one Indian working for him, F. Kingsbury, one of the translators of the Śaivite hymns.[129] In addition, several of the Christian authors of The Heritage of India Series were in some capacity involved in the movement towards Church union in south India.

It is perhaps for all these reasons, and given the visibility of Hooper in the Church Union Movement, that Farquhar (and V.S. Azariah too) settled on the Wesleyan Methodist minister to translate the āḻvār poems as a kind of companion volume to the 1921 Tamil Śaiva poems. Given that as far as we know Hooper did not produce any further work on Tamil religious literature (apart from his overview of Bible translations in Tamil and other Indian vernaculars), it is likely that his engagement with āḻvār poetry was more one of contingency than a lifelong affair. In his preface to the *Hymns of the Ālvārs*, Hooper recognizes as much, admitting that he was urged to take on the project by Farquhar; he also acknowledges two Śrīvaiṣṇava men for their assistance with the manuscript.[130] It is hard to assess what Hooper's Tamil-language competency was, or how deeply he understood the Tamil literary world. The brief 1934 review of *Hymns of the Ālvārs* in the *Journal of the Royal Asiatic Society of Great Britain and Ireland* finds Hooper's book to be wanting. This review by F.J. Richards considers four books from The Heritage of India Series and two from The Religious Life of India Series. In it, he compares Hooper's work unfavourably with H.A. Popley's lucid survey of Indian music and his translation of the *Tirukkuṟaḷ*, which, incidentally, he finds to be a worthy sequel to G.U. Pope's (1820–1908) translation. While F.J. Richards makes no mention of the general quality of the translation, he finds the information on the dating of the āḻvār both incomplete and deficient, and the history of Vaiṣṇavism lacking clarity.[131] In this latter assessment, the reviewer is largely correct, although Hooper's introduction accurately summarizes the major contours of the debates surrounding the dating of the āḻvārs, and offers his own judgements.[132] The review makes no mention of the tastefully chosen Vaiṣṇava images that grace the opening pages of the book, or that Hooper offers copious notes on each of the poems he chooses to translate. All of this ancillary material enhances the translation, and demonstrates a desire to provide something of a living context to the poems. In his introduction, Hooper describes the annual Mārkaḻi Adhyāyanotsavam in Srirangam and the role of the Araiyars in liturgical recitations of the entire *Nālāyira Divya Prabandham.*[133]

Some fifty years later, Friedhelm Hardy largely agrees with Richards's review and dismisses Hooper's translation and the accompanying explanations of the *Tiruviruttam* as missing the point of the poem. In Hardy's estimation, Hooper doesn't acknowledge what the *Tiruviruttam* owes to its literary antecedents—true enough—and therefore fails to know how to proceed in his interpretation.[134] He acknowledges that Hooper is guided in his brief notes by the commentators, but since the commentators themselves were unaware of the Caṅkam past (according to Hardy), the errors of our intrepid translator are somewhat deflected. All of this is largely in keeping with one of Hardy's central arguments in *Viraha-Bhakti* that the emergence of the Śrīvaiṣṇava commentarial tradition stifles the ecstatic, experiential and expressive elements of Tamil Vaiṣṇava bhakti. But as we have seen in the discussions above, commentators like Periyavāccāṉ Piḷḷai were not unaware of the Caṅkam past; rather, their focus was elsewhere, and they were guided by different aesthetic imperatives. In recent years, Frank Clooney, John Carman and Vasudha Narayanan have all argued sensitively for the need to take the commentators' readings of these poems seriously.[135]

As early as 1929, Hooper had certainly recognized the value of the Śrīvaiṣṇavas' exegetical tradition and he strove to incorporate the commentators' voice into his translation. It is hard to tell if this impulse was guided by his difficulty with the text or on the guidance of two learned advisers,

Govindacharya Svamin and S. Vasudevachariar, the bursar of Wesley College; the former seems to have directed him to the *Ācārya Hṛdayam*. Although Hooper doesn't cite the *Ācārya Hṛdayam*, he provides a translation from what he claims is an anonymous Sanskrit text which provides detailed allegorical concordances for the characters and other elements that occur in āḻvār poetry. Of using this work Hooper says, 'The understanding of sacred erotic poetry is simplified if generally accepted esoteric meaning of recurring symbols is held in mind.'[136]

Hooper's decision to include the *Tiruviruttam* instead of selections from the *Tiruvāymoḻi* demonstrates his primary interest in showcasing that which is unusual about Tamil Vaiṣṇava poetry. In addition, the ability to present a text in its entirety so as to convey a 'consecutive view of the qualities of the hymns' was also clearly important to him.[137] He does not of course translate all of the *Tiruviruttam*; missing are several verses, but there doesn't seem to be any discernible logic for their omission.[138] Nonetheless, Hooper sees the *Tiruviruttam* as representative of Nammāḻvār's poetry.[139] He notes that the poem is obscure and difficult, and correctly identifies that it is inconsistent in maintaining its personae and fails to adhere to any notion of consecutive action. Hooper, though, is clearly puzzled by these elements and explains them away by asking the reader to simply imagine that the lover comes and goes between verses.[140] For all these drawbacks—and the translation in stilted four-line English verse is the most obvious one—Hooper is sensitive to the poem's dual architecture. Each translated verse is accompanied by a colophon of sorts in which he provides the literary situation, and in some cases its metaphysical counterpart within parentheses. Here is his colophon for *Tiruviruttam* 2 followed by his translation:

The maid speaks, seeing the state of her mistress, unable to endure separation from her lord, who has left her. (Here the maid stands for the Āḻvār's disciples, the mistress for the Āḻvār, the lord for Vishnu).

Long may she love, this girl with luring locks,
Who loves the feet that heavenly ones adore,
The feet of Kaṇṇan, dark as rainy clouds:
Her red eyes all abrim with tears of grief,
Like darting Kayal fish in a deep pool.[141]

The translation is heavily annotated, although the notes are quite brief. He offers single-line sentences on the significance of the feet (line 2), and the name Kaṇṇa<u>n</u> (line 3), explains the logic of the simile of the fish-like eyes, glosses the 'heavenly ones' as *nitya*s (that is, nityasūri), then cautions the reader to banish any correlation of red eyes to weeping (line 4), and guides them to associate it with high passion instead. Hooper's translation is very much a product of its time, not just in its ponderous English rendition but more importantly in all its accompanying apparatus of introduction, notes and annotation, and well in keeping with the stated mission of Farquhar's The Heritage of India Series.

Exactly fifty years later, Prema Nandakumar, a prominent Indian scholar and translator, published a translation (or rather transcreation) of the *Tiruviruttam* under the title *Nammāḻvār's 'Tiruviruttam': The Drama of the Love Divine.* This transcreation emerges out of the Writers' Workshop, a working group founded in 1958 in Calcutta with the express purpose of integrating English into India's cultural ethos.[142] Nandakumar's effort is accompanied by a brief introduction that charts the correspondence developed in the commentarial traditions between each of Nammāḻvār's four poems and their respective Vedic counterparts. Within this framework, the *Tiruviruttam* is regarded as the equivalent of the *Ṛg Veda*. The translation itself is careful to adhere to the four-line verse format of the *Tiruviruttam*, with brief headers that condense the poem's primary akapporuḷ content: He on Her eyes, Bless the Night, She on Her Heart, and so forth. The headers succeed in conveying the dramatic and dialogic qualities of the *Tiruviruttam* (hence Nandakumar's title), and ultimately work to weave the poem into a continuous narrative with the final verse (phala śruti) of the poem titled 'Consummation'. An example of her English transcreation is as follows:

25 SHE ON HIS GARLAND

Beloved of Him who's greater than Brahma
Lord of all gods. His *tulasī* garland
Has caused the loosening of my bangles,
And there's no end to the harm it can do.[143]

The great translator of Indian literary works, A.K. Ramanujan, brought his own unique and extraordinary aesthetic sensibilities to the *Tiruviruttam* in *Hymns for the Drowning*, published a mere two years after Prema Nandakumar's Writers' Workshop transcreation. As was typical of Ramanujan, he chose those poems that spoke to him and selected just seven verses from the *Tiruviruttam* that he identified as being in the classical mode.[144] Six of them (7, 11, 12, 16, 60 and 68) appear in the book's section entitled 'Four Returning Voices' and *Tiruviruttam* 94 rounds out the selection provocatively designated 'Questions'. The arrangement of the translated verses is meant to invite contemplation of the inter-animation of the individual verses, and between the *Tiruviruttam* and *Tiruvāymoḻi*. In this, Ramanujan is certainly influenced by the tradition's own intertextual reading and interpretive practices, and his radial approach to interpreting Indic texts.[145] Further, the verses are organized to mimic the alternation between philosophical sections and other kinds of verses that is a hallmark of the *Tiruvāymoḻi*, and hints of which you see in the *Tiruviruttam* as well. In Ramanujan's arrangement, the six *Tiruviruttam* verses are placed towards the end of the narrative progression and occur right before the verses from the *Tiruvāymoḻi* depicting what he termed 'mutual cannibalism'. The *Tiruviruttam* translations in *Hymns for the Drowning* are beautiful, moving poems in their own right. In keeping with his minimalist translation style, unadorned by punctuation, the English words flow down the page evocative of unrestrained emotion. The Nammāḻvār verses (especially those in the akam mode) hark back to their Caṅkam ancestors and Ramanujan's own initial translation efforts of those old Tamil love poems with the headers that he made standard:

What She Said:
Skin dark as young mango leaf
  is wilting.
Yellow patched spread all over me.
Night is as long as several lives.

All these are the singular dowry
my good heart brings
as she goes over
to the cool basil

of my lord, the Dark One
with the wheel that cuts down demons.

Tiruviruttam 12[146]

Srirama Bharati (1949–2000), most famous for his reimagining of Araiyar Cēvai, the Śrīvaiṣṇava hereditary ritual practice, published a bilingual translation of the entire *Nālāyira Divya Prabandham* in 2000. The book was brought out under the aegis of the trust he founded, the Sri Sadagopan Tirunarayanaswami Divya Prabandha Pathasala in Jaladampettai, a suburb of Madras. The purpose of the trust (which includes the Tirunarayanaswami Temple) was to reacquaint Śrīvaiṣṇavas with the works of the āḻvārs and to thus inculcate a virtuous life. Attendant to this effort was Bharati's interest in 'reviving' Araiyar Cēvai, a form he saw as dying out. Renaming it *devagāṉam* (divine music), he reconstituted Araiyar Cēvai and styled himself as an Araiyar under the title Selvamudaiyanpettai Araiyar. Bharati's English translation of the *Nālāyira Divya Prabandham* bears the distinct imprint of these twin concerns. The blurb on the back of the book informs us that Bharati is from a family of scholars and that the present work is the result of over twenty-five years of deep contemplation on the words of the āḻvārs and the ācāryas. And, crucially, Bharati is identified on the blurb and on the book's front page both by his given name (Srirama Bharati) and his performative identity of Selvamudaiyanpettai Araiyar. Although regular editions of the *Divya Prabandham* are not published with associated *paṇ* (tunes) like the *Tēvāram*, Bharati, in keeping with his concern for the performative dimensions of the āḻvār compositions as songs, identifies a *rāga* and *tāla* for each decad (tirumoḻi). This is Bharati's own innovation, and the textualization of his reimagined Araiyar Cēvai as devagāṉam. However, since the *Tiruviruttam* falls under the Iyaṟpā, or the so-called prose section of the *Divya Prabandham*, he assigns neither rāga nor tāla to the individual verses. Visually, the English text follows below the Tamil, with the sequence of alternating Tamil–English verses set into two tight columns. No artificial breaks of text, identification of speakers or assignments of musical modes and rhythms intervene, and the entire *Tiruviruttam* (including the single *taṉiyaṉ*, or laudatory verse) is rendered into simple, serviceable prose. The following is a typical translation, and his debt to the commentarial tradition is evident. I have not reproduced the Tamil.

> The lord is the antidote for the venom of evil Karmas and manna for good deeds. He is the bridegroom of the goddess on the lotus. Without belittling himself, he grazed cows and protected them. Then in the yore he strode the Earth in two steps. Alas, when will we attain him? (89)[147]

Crossing the Wastelands: Some Thoughts on Translating the *Tiruviruttam*

My translation of the *Tiruviruttam* is in many ways utterly accidental. I first read the *Tiruviruttam* deeply over the course of a year around 2007 for two reasons: I was interested in the use of the female voice in āḻvār poetry, and I was working on the ritual performance repertoire of Nammāḻvār's temple in Alvar Tirunagari. At this time, I was more concerned with the *Tiruviruttam*'s commentaries than the poem itself, for this is what translated itself into the ritual performances at Alvar

Tirunagari.[148] The poem failed to capture my attention, and I recall labouring through it, veering between confusion and frustration most of the time. The only anubhava was one of pain and discomfort. The exhilaration I had felt when I first encountered Āṇṭāḷ or Tirumaṅkai's *Periya Tirumoḻi* was completely absent. Although I found individual verses of the *Tiruviruttam* arresting, I could discern no structure, no logic to the text beyond what the commentators had so carefully laid out. Nevertheless, I dutifully translated the poem in service of these other projects and began annotating it, guided primarily by Periyavāccāṉ Piḷḷai's commentarial genius. But, as I lived with this poem for six years, compelled to return to it over and over again, sometimes just a verse at a time for several days, my understanding of it began to unfurl, hesitant and shy as the first new buds of spring. The poem slowly but surely began to assume a new shape and new sound in English. The translation become a sort of yoga, a self-discipline I imposed on myself to enter into the skin of the poem, to inhabit its strange, mysterious, many-limbed body, and through the exegesis of translation to create and finally experience anubhava. It is the symbiotic experiential dimension of anubhava that has guided this translation, a work that is in every way *my* anubhava grantha on Nammāḻvār's *Tiruviruttam*.

In its new figuration as my anubhava grantha, the first things to go were some of the *Tiruviruttam*'s distinctive formal features: head-rhymes, rhyming in general, metre and, of course, the antāti. The poem is rendered into free verse, but this does not mean I have been insensitive to its internal rhythms or that the lines are arranged arbitrarily. I have chosen a style that approximates the tight, dense structure of the poem, where the vocabulary is straightforward, but their use and the ideas they express are profound. For the most part, I have kept the lines in translated English short, the vocabulary simple (īṉaccol), and I have happily embraced contractions, for instance in *Tiruviruttam* 14.

He Said:

Are her two eyes
spears that cut through me
or lovely fish that illumine my life
and don't draw back?

Are they radiant arrows of divine Kāma?
Or are these enchanting eyes two kayal
searching for the city of the lord
whose form is a brilliant dark fire?

While the aforementioned word density of the *Tiruviruttam* lent itself readily to a suitable English form, the antāti proved a formidable obstacle to resolve in translation. In Nammāḻvār's hands, the antāti is forged through a supple use of homonyms, puns and a masterful manipulation of syllabic sound. He deploys these to make significant theological arguments about the never-ending cycle of lovers' union and separation; of Viṣṇu's nature as the universe's cause and its end; of the endless cycle of birth and death from which only Viṣṇu can offer release; and the poem, which has neither beginning nor end, thus becomes the very embodiment of Viṣṇu's unfathomable nature. There can be no argument that this is one of the distinctive formal features of the poem, and ideally one ought to be able to reproduce it in translation. But the multiple ways in which Nammāḻvār employs the antāti—where the same word is used at the end and beginning; where the same sound is used (homonyms); or, in still other cases, where only one part/syllable of the word is used—are close to impossible to reproduce without sacrificing comprehensibility. The wordplay in the *Tiruviruttam*, common in Nammāḻvār's poetry and undoubtedly one of the pleasures of the text, is an insurmountable hurdle, and one for which I was unable to find a sufficiently satisfying solution. As a result, I arrived at several compromises and alternatives. Wherever possible (when the word or phrase is duplicated) I follow the antāti, but in other instances I have sought recourse to other strategies and rhetorical devices—assonance, consonance, alliteration have been stalwart companions—to convey the *feeling* of the antāti, if not its formal features. I have made no attempt to link each individual verse as tightly as Nammāḻvār does in the *Tiruviruttam*, and have instead let subtler links (such as repeated motifs and myths) speak their own connections.

There are other features of the poem that have been easier to approximate. For the most part, each translated verse adheres to the order of the Tamil's four-line verse. That is, rather than reverse the word order as is often the case because of Tamil's so-called left-branching syntax to accommodate English's right-branching one, I have, for the most part, retained line order if not word order. This has been made easier by the structure of each individual verse, which generally posits a proposition in its opening two lines, and what I call a (re)turn in its closing two lines. While there was no way to keep the four-line structure without compromising intelligibility, I have rendered each verse as having two distinct parts. I have avoided punctuations wherever possible in the first part of the verse to indicate continuity of thought and idea between its proposition and return. So, although each verse is divided into two parts, these are not meant to be taken as two separate stanzas.

In the Śrīvaiṣṇava commentarial tradition, the *Tiruviruttam*'s two complementary layers—the exoteric (anyāpadeśa) and the esoteric (svāpadeśa)—are essential to guiding any faithful reading/rendering of the text. The exoteric is expressed in the poem's literary architecture, in its slow unfolding of the narrative of love between the anonymous male and female leads. This carefully constructed literary plan serves to make the poet's profound esotericism palpable. According to the poem's traditional interpreters, only thoughtful, deliberate contemplation of the interpenetration of the literary and the theological will reveal the *Tiruviruttam*'s central arguments. In some instances, the interpenetration of the erotic and esoteric planes is so complete that it is hard to distinguish one from the other. *Tiruviruttam* 84 illustrates this beautifully, where the love-longing of the heroine echoes the same intense feeling of the poet. In Tamil:

taiyal nallārkaḷ kuḻāṅkaḷ kuḻiya kuḻuviṉullām
aiya nallārkaḷ kuḻiya viḻaviṉum aṅku aṅku ellām
kaiya poṉ āḻiveṇ caṅkōṭum kāṇpāṉ avāvuvaṉ nāṉ
maiya vaṇṇā maṇiyē muttamē entaṉ māṇikkamē

In English, in this very early draft:

Amidst a throng of lovely women or
in a crowd of virtuous priests
in some festival, or in places here and there
with the golden disc and white conch in your hands
I desire to see you
O dark one, precious gem, pearl
my dear glittering ruby.

In early versions of my translation, the verse appeared as above, aligned with the page's left margin. But any translation of the *Tiruviruttam* has to be sensitive to the poem's dual architecture, to its mansion of many apartments. One way to demonstrate the implied relationship between the outer and the inner, between akam and puṟam, between anyāpadeśa and svāpadeśa, is to demarcate the inner space of the poem through the verbal and visual markers that identify each verse's speaker. In the final version the same verse looks like this on the page:

She Said:

> Amidst a throng of lovely women
> or surrounded by crowds of virtuous priests
> in some festival or in places like that
>
> I long to see you
> holding in your hands golden disc and white conch
> O one dark as kohl my precious gem
> pearl of mine my glittering ruby.

I draw attention to the akapporuḷ frame by identifying the verse's speaker (She Said) in an indented header. This indented header also acts as a visual reminder that the poem's speakers act within a frame. The body of the translated verse is then further indented to suggest its own interiority—the svāpadeśa within the anyāpadeśa. In those instances where the frame is ruptured (*Tiruviruttam* 1, 21, 99, 100), the translation follows the poem's lead. No speakers are identified and the translated verse remains un-indented and flush with the left margin, evoking visually the inner heart of the poem making itself known and visible.

The poem's last ten verses presented a problem as one might regard this final section as the poem's masterfully orchestrated dénouement, in which the interior and exterior planes come together. I have reflected this coming together by identifying the speaker of the verse as the heroine (so staying true to the akam context) and instead of indenting the translation as in all the previous akam verses, the verse aligns with this identifying header, and they both appear flush with the left margin.

The two possession/revelation verses, *Tiruviruttam* 48 and 94, by their very curious character stick out in the poem. They are, in a way, inversions of the poem's very pretext. In these two verses, the poem is no longer a viṇṇappam, but god's own words. The poet and deity through their shared words and shared anubhava are mirrors to the other, at least momentarily. To invoke all of this, I have aligned *Tiruviruttam* 48 and 94 with the right margin to draw the eye to the dramatic manner in which the verses break the frame, and to displace the reader's acceptance of the poem's pretext.

To enhance these cues that make visible the *Tiruviruttam*'s structure and play, the translated verses run together. However, I have not allowed a translated verse to be divided on account of a page break. Leaving a single verse on a page (in the manner of A.K. Ramanujan's *Hymns for the Drowning*) was tempting. Individual verses are enigmatic enough to invite sustained thinking. Several of the verses (or lines) from the *Tiruviruttam* are cited individually in commentaries and in ritual performances, so such an approach would not really violate how the poem is used and experienced by Śrīvaiṣṇavas. Nonetheless, having sacrificed the antāti, I felt it was important to preserve the integrity of the *Tiruviruttam* in other ways. Eventually I decided that the reading experience of the poem and visual impact of the translation would be more effective if the verses run together as opposed to standing alone. The only exceptions are verses 1 and 100, which are placed on a single page each. There are two reasons for this decision. The first is to draw attention to their framing function. But, more importantly, I wanted to find a way to set these two verses, which are both the poem's beginning and its end, bound as they are by their antāti, into fruitful conversation. Hence, not only are these two verses on individual pages, but they also do not adhere to the two-part structure that I have applied to the rest of the verses.

Nammāḻvār's poetic style is one that favours brevity and tightness. It makes for verses that glow as though lit from the inside like a flawless gem of concentrated colour. Like many great Tamil poets, he achieves this effect with a breathless cascade of striking images, metaphors and sounds that in the Tamil script quite literally run into each other. This is a key feature of the experience of reciting the *Tiruviruttam*. It evokes breath-taking, not just on account of its sumptuous use of language, but because as you read or recite the poem, you are often left trying to seize your breath. In Tamil, the poem recreates the heady sense of mystical experience, and its use of language draws attention to your breath, your uyir, the oscillations of breathing in and out mimicking the filling and emptying that characterizes the peculiar relish of such an experience. This is perhaps one of the most stunning features of the poem and one I felt was integral to Nammāḻvār's poetic vision, as significant as the antāti. Thus I have kept punctuation to an absolute minimum, and have avoided placing commas between strings of epithets or adjectives. This violation of the rules of English grammar is meant to recreate the rush of feeling that the Tamil torrent of words produces in the hearer and listener. You are supposed to be left breathless and slightly dazed after each verse, overcome by the sheer lushness of sounds and images, for that is the affect that Nammāḻvār's original ingeniously produces.

There are several words in Tamil that are so richly polyvalent that no single English word can accurately capture its range. The words *vi<u>n</u>ai* (deed, action, the result of accumulated karma, by extension, fate) and aruḷ (grace, mercy, compassion, favour, benevolence) occur frequently in the poem in various grammatical forms. Gesturing to its import, aruḷ occurs in the very first verse (*aruḷāy*: be gracious) of the *Tiruviruttam*. In the case of vi<u>n</u>ai, it often occurs as a participle noun—like *valvi<u>n</u>aiyē<u>n</u>* (I who have terrible deeds)—that describes the wretchedness of the first-person speaker. It is also meant to convey the sense of being caught in the web of deeds that has a determinative effect on one's present condition. I toyed with offering context-sensitive translations of vi<u>n</u>ai and its variants, but in the end felt this failed to do justice to the power that builds around the word with Nammāḻvār's deliberate and effective use. Although not a direct or literal translation, and in many ways an inadequate one, I ultimately chose to render vi<u>n</u>ai as fate. This is partly because phrases like valvi<u>n</u>aiyē<u>n</u> (I who have terrible deeds) become terribly clunky in English, not to mention somewhat incomprehensible. More importantly, these translated phrases simply fail to convey the speaker's profound helplessness and deep horror that the word vi<u>n</u>ai evokes in him. Fate conveys a similar sense with its connotation of an inexorable hold over the direction of one's life, and I ultimately chose it for the power it produces with its one short hard-hitting syllable. I have consistently translated vi<u>n</u>ai as fate throughout the poem, and the reader will be able to index its occurrences against its entire complex range of meanings.

Aruḷ (grace, benevolence, mercy, compassion, favour) posed equally difficult problems. Aside from the Christian overtones that the word grace elicits, aruḷ is a kind of dynamic connection that moves between god and devotee. In these bhakti poems, aruḷ is often described in aqueous terms, as cooling, liquid, unbounded, flowing. No word in English can convey all of this. So although I began with the opposite approach to viṉai, rendering the word aruḷ differently each time depending on the context to convey its full breadth of meanings, in the end I found it to be a self-defeating proposition. Rather than bringing out the range of possibilities of the word aruḷ, the translation began to fragment around this very important concept—mercy warring with compassion warring with grace. After several iterations, I settled on an imperfect choice—grace—as it has the widest possible semantic net of the other possible choices. There was another more compelling reason for choosing this word above others. The *Tiruviruttam* draws one's attention repeatedly to Viṣṇu's eyes, to his gaze and glance.[149] The heroine rejoices in the beauty of his eyes, the poet begs for his glance, revels in the cool caress of his gaze. In the world of the *Tiruviruttam* (and indeed the world of Tamil bhakti), to be bathed in the gaze of god is to receive aruḷ. Grace, with its visual and aural closeness to gaze/glance, successfully evokes this expressive, dynamic, intimate and sensory quality of aruḷ as mediated through the eye (I). Again, I have used the word grace consistently throughout the *Tiruviruttam* as a translation for aruḷ and its grammatical variants.

I have left Tamil- or Sanskrit-derived words for flora and fauna untranslated, except when they have a well-known English equivalent, lotus being one such exception. Wherever a more familiar Indic equivalent exists (tulasī for tuḻāy), I have used it. I rejected using basil for tuḻāy although it belongs to the same family of plants, as it tends to evoke for most American and European English speakers the large-leafed, sweet-smelling basil used in Italian and Thai cooking, rather than the small-leaved, slightly sharp-tasting strain that one finds in south India. After much oscillation, I have chosen not to italicize untranslated Tamil and Sanskrit words, like tulasī. Rather than draw attention to their foreignness, this choice naturalizes their occurrence within the poem, avoiding an unnecessary visual disruption. In many cases, the verse will clarify the untranslated word, such as in verse 2, where it becomes clear that *kayal* refers to a native freshwater fish:

Her eyes with their fine red lines
    dart like kayal in a full pond
O let her live
that woman with dense curly hair

her love adorns the feet
of Kaṇṇaṉ dark as heavy rain clouds
worshipped by the ancient ones
who live in the sky.

I have also left all Viṣṇu's names untranslated and in their Tamil forms, thus Madhusūdaṉaṉ as opposed to the 'killer of Madhu' or Madhusūdana. For Sanskrit-derived names, I have retained a transliteration that reflects the Sanskrit rather than the Tamil as it is more familiar and easier to read (so Mādhavaṉ instead of Mātavaṉ). An index of Viṣṇu's names used in the *Tiruviruttam* can be found in Appendix 3. I have also provided a glossary of Indic words that appear in the introduction and in the poem itself.

Over six years, as I sat with this difficult, vexing, profound poem, trying to make it resonate in English, the *Tiruviruttam* gradually lost its opacity. Still, as I doggedly journeyed through the arid, dreadful pālai of misinterpretation, like Kaṇṇaṉ's glorious Veḥkā with its rich, verdant, honey-filled groves, the paradise of the perfect translation danced like a mirage, ever out of reach. The *Tiruviruttam* posed unique challenges and ones that went beyond the (almost) insurmountable ones of language and aesthetic sensibilities that separate Tamil devotional poetry and contemporary English. But, ultimately, in the crossover from Tamil into English, in trying to go beyond inelegant verbal equivalences, the poem's moving parts revealed themselves. As I forced myself to dissect this living, breathing, chimerical poem, to atomize it if you will, it bared itself (even as it hid so much): its minutiae of syntax, its sinews of metaphors, its muscles of the mythic. Then, it became something else, the translation alive with its own new grammar, animated by its own tensile connective tissues, a text of breath, feeling and emotion. In the end, although I endeavoured to be accurate, to stay as close to Nammāḻvār's original, this translation owes as much to my long engagement with āḻvār poetry as it does to the long list of great translators of Indic poetry—George Hart, Steven Hopkins, A.K. Ramanujan, Martha Selby, David Shulman loom large here—who first drew me into the luminous world of Tamil poetry. And to John Keats, my companion soul-poet whose poetry never fails to silence me like stout Cortez upon a peak in Darien.

PART III

PERIYAVĀCCA<u>N</u> PIḶḶAI'S COMMENTARY ON THE *TIRUVIRUTTAM*

What follow are brief summaries of Periyavāccā<u>n</u> Piḷḷai's commentary for six verses from the *Tiruviruttam*. I have chosen one representative verse for each of the main characters in the poem (heroine, hero, heroine's friend and the mother), the first purely *svāpadeśa* verse of the poem (21), and the important commentary for the *Tiruviruttam*'s penultimate verse (99).

These paraphrases follow the lead of John Carman and Vasudha Narayanan's *The Tamil Veda: Piḷḷā<u>n</u>'s Interpretation of the Tiruvāymoḻi*. The fourth section of their book provides translations of selected verses from the *Tiruvāymoḻi* accompanied by a brief synopsis of the commentator's main interpretive points.

My aim is to provide a taste of Periyavāccā<u>n</u> Piḷḷai's imaginative and creative engagements with the *Tiruviruttam*. I have not attempted to chart a detailed theological reading of the *Tiruviruttam*, or to offer a translation of Piḷḷai's commentaries for these selected verses. In this spirit, I have kept my interjections to the bare minimum, and my observations (when they occur) are marked by a direct reference to Piḷḷai or to the commentary in general. My comments are generally placed to provide continuity or context. However, the majority of the text below reflects Periyavāccā<u>n</u> Piḷḷai's interpretation.

There are several sources in Tamil and English that undertake a more exhaustive philosophical interpretation of the poem at hand. Recent publications in English that offer a traditional commentary on the text include K.R. Krishnaswami, *Iyarpa: 4000 Divya Prabandam* Series, Vol. 8 (Bangalore: A&K Prakashana, 2010), and the e-book by Oppiliappan Koil Sri Varadachari Sathakopan, *Thiruviruttham and Rg Vedam*, http://www.sadagopan.org/index.php/categories/doc_details/241-ss083-thiruviruttham-synopsis.

Tiruviruttam 21

Celestials in the sky
offer you pure perfect garlands anoint you with cool water
worship you with beautiful incense

you vanish by a trick

to scoop up and eat butter
to dance between the two sharp horns
of the humped bull
for the lovely woman of the strong cowherd clan.

In the previous verse (*Tiruviruttam* 20), the heroine had swooned, but her friend awakened her in time to interrupt the Vēlan̲'s misguided activities. There, she recommends a more efficacious medicine, namely, the chanting of Viṣṇu's names and the offering of the garland. The *āḻvār* upon hearing these words (uttered in the previous verse—the lord who swallowed the seven worlds) is brought back to himself and utters these lines.

This verse is also concerned with the twin attributes of Viṣṇu—his transcendence (*paratvam*) and his accessibility (*saulabhyam*). The first two lines are set in Vaikuṇṭha, where Viṣṇu is happily enjoying the services of his eternal devotees, the *nityasūris*. But suddenly, overwhelmed by the desire to taste the butter churned by his devotees, he manifests on earth (*līlā vibhūti*) in his *vibhāva avatāra* as Kṛṣṇa.

If one wonders why Nammāḻvār chose to celebrate the Kṛṣṇa avatāra instead of the Rāma avatāra, Periyavāccān̲ Piḷḷai suggests that Nammāḻvār is naturally attracted to the former. This is why when he awakens from the swoon, he immediately calls Kṛṣṇa to mind.

Nammāḻvār demonstrates Viṣṇu's compassion for his devotee with two illustrative episodes. The first is the stealing of the butter and the second is Kṛṣṇa's marriage to Nappiṉṉai.

Piḷḷai's commentary begins with a reference to the first verse of the *Tiruvāymoḻi* (I.1.1), where god is shown in his transcendent, abstract form. This is how *Tiruviruttam* 21 also begins. In *Tiruvāymoḻi* I.2.1, Nammāḻvār establishes the means (*upāya*) to achieve *mokṣa*. Finally, in I.3.1, he demonstrates god's accessibility through the Kṛṣṇa avatāra. In this manner, Piḷḷai suggests that *Tiruviruttam* 21 can be seen to condense the ideas developed in the first three decads of the *Tiruvāymoḻi*, which move the reader from a meditation on god's transcendence to a contemplation of his immanent presence.

Tiruviruttam 37

The Mother Said:

For many years I worshipped
Kaṇṇaṉ's glorious feet adorned with flowers.
I was blessed
with this tender fawn-like girl whose waist is slender.
I am ill-fated.

She's taken the wide forest path
where hunters with curved bows
cattle rustlers murderous bandits
and fleet-footed youth beat drums
like the gossip of village women.

In the *anyāpadeśa* interpretation, this verse is spoken by the girl's mother (*tāy*), who discovers that her daughter has left home unexpectedly. She is unsure whether the girl has eloped with the hero or she has simply followed him out of her desperate longing. Piḷḷai likens the mother in this verse to her persona in *Tiruvāymoḻi* VI.7, but with a key difference. In VI.7 the mother knows where the girl has gone—Tirukkolur—while here she is left unaware.

The descriptions of the various dangers of the wasteland afford Piḷḷai the opportunity to explore the nature of god. He says, while these cattle rustlers steal cattle and cause harm, Viṣṇu (as the cowherd) only protects them. These strange men kill neither for money nor for enmity, but simply for pleasure. However, Viṣṇu kills only out of necessity, and even when he does so, the offender attains mokṣa.

In his discussion of the dangers of the wasteland, Piḷḷai offers an odd reference to the youth who keep themselves fit by using *rasāyana*, an oblique reference to alchemy, and perhaps Siddha practices.

Piḷḷai lavishes attention on the mother's utterance, *aruvin̲aiyēn̲*—I who have difficult/terrible deeds, which I have translated as 'I am ill-fated'. He provides a multi-tiered explanation for the mother's use of this phrase. First, the daughter knowing that the mother would disapprove of her love affair has chosen to run away. Second, instead of helping unite the lovers, the mother acted as an obstacle. In this, Piḷḷai compares the mother to Bharata in the Rāmāyaṇa, who blames himself for Rāma's exile. Finally, he compares the mother of this wayward girl to Devakī, who observed several vows to earn Kṛṣṇa as her son, only to be separated from him.

In the svāpadeśa, the āl̲vār is seen as abandoning *saṁsāra* which no longer interests him.

Tiruviruttam 46

She Said:

Some send their heart as a messenger
to do their bidding
thinking 'It's an innocent heart, it's *my* heart.'
They should abandon such notions.

My steadfast heart left to place a message
at the feet of the one
who ripped the broad chest of the golden one
but it abandoned me, wanders even now.

In the anyāpadeśa, this verse is spoken by the heroine (*talaivi*).

The commentary for this verse is an explication of the nature of the relationship of the devotee's heart and god. The central question is: why does the āl̲vār praise the heart (*vāl̲i maṭa neñcē*) in *Tiruviruttam* 45 only to immediately chastise it in this verse? The answer is that the heart is both the reason for bondage in this world and the means to be released from it. Therefore, the heart causes despair and pain. It whips up the emotions, takes the devotee to the very final point, but abandons the quest at the crucial juncture without reconciling the god and the heroine. But isn't the heart also the cause of the union? That is, is it not the heart that provides the reason and the motivation to seek union? Piḷḷai answers in the negative, because the heart can only function as an aid (*upākārakan̲*). God is the only cause and instigator (*karaṇan̲*). The heart is needed because it desires the *puruṣārtha*s (the 'goals of life', but in the context of the commentary it is understood as mokṣa). It is merely instrumental in securing fulfilment, but it is by no means the primary or essential reason.

We think of the heart as our own, but it is not the case. Viṣṇu gave us a body in order to apprehend the world, and with this he gave us the senses that are for both knowing and acting in this world. The heart resides in the body; it is a *śeṣa* (servant) and is to be used as such.

Piḷḷai offers two illustrative examples to discuss the relationships of the heart to the devotee and of the heart to god. In the first, he compares the heroine to Prahlāda who was tormented by Hiraṇya, his father, yet remained steadfast in his devotion to Viṣṇu. The heart is Hiraṇya, who betrayed a natural relationship to tread an evil path. Similarly, in this verse, the heart has abandoned the heroine, yet she must remain single-minded in her love for Viṣṇu. Given the allusion to the Narasiṁha myth in the verse, it is no surprise that Piḷḷai chooses it to embellish his primary concern, which is the nature of the heart's relationship to the devotee and to god. The second example is taken from Piḷḷai's favourite, the *Vālmīki Rāmāyaṇa*. He parallels the heroine's state to the second separation between Rāma and Sītā, where although she was abandoned and waited patiently, Rāma remained steadfast in his course of action.

Tiruviruttam 50

He Said:

O skilled charioteer, drive quickly
Take me to her of the lustrous brow
before her colour fades

Take me to the great mountain
where waterfalls crash on the foothills
like strings of pearls from the tall crown of
Vaikuṇṭha's master,
one sweet as nectar.

In the anyāpadeśa reading of this verse, Piḷḷai tells us that the hero (*talaivaṉ*) urges his charioteer to return him to the heroine in order to preserve her beauty and his honour. In the time they have been separated, memories of her beauty have sustained him; he is like Rāma during Sītā's captivity. The beauty of her forehead shores up his spirits like the small package of food one takes on a journey. He wants to return to his love quickly for he knows she will not survive, like Rāma hurrying back to Ayodhya from exile, well aware that Bharata's life hung in the balance.

Once again, the poet meditates on the contrast of Viṣṇu in his transcendent form (evoked here through the phrase *viṇ-mutal*: cause/first of Vaikuṇṭha) and in his accessible, local form (*māmalaikku*—to the great mountain). Piḷḷai asks why the poet invokes Viṣṇu in his transcendent aspect, but then chooses to go to the great mountain, a local site? Nammāḻvār's thoughts are solely fixed on his form in Vaikuṇṭha, and he describes the great mountain (note that he doesn't specify a specific mountainous site like Venkatam in this verse) according to his apprehension of that world. In this world one can only understand god's nature through sight, but when one experiences him, one can intuit that nature. This is like seeing the smoke from a forest fire and deducing that there is a fire on the mountain.

In the svāpadeśa for this verse, the heart is the chariot. It describes the *bhāgavatas* (Nammāḻvār's assembled disciples) rushing to Nammāḻvār's aid on account of his suffering. The poet has forgotten saṁsāra and this world and has a single-minded focus only on the lord of Vaikuṇṭha, like Sītā who forgot Mithila upon arriving in Ayodhya.

Tiruviruttam 74

Her Friend Said:

His long eyes closed, he slumbers
upon his bed resting
on rolling rising ocean waves
When he comes awake
he swallows worlds

A fresh gentle breeze wafts
having devoured the fragrance of tulasī
adorning the crown of that same one
who uprooted the great mountain
turned it on its head.

In this verse the heroine's friend (*tōḻi*) comforts her when the cool breeze arrives. Recognizing her despair, the friend says that this is no ordinary breeze, but one that comes bearing the fragrance of Viṣṇu's *tulasī*. This must surely mean that Viṣṇu is not far behind. After all, doesn't the fragrance of sandalwood herald a king's arrival? This is why the breeze is described as fresh—as it stops nowhere on its way to the heroine, it is unpolluted with the fragrance of other, lesser things.

Viṣṇu's eyes are lovely and long because they speak of his greatness. He is not truly asleep, instead he is in a deep meditation (*yoga nidrā*), considering the protection, creation and destruction of the world. Even so, he is right at hand at the time of dissolution (*pralaya*) to take care of his devotees. This is why at the time of pralaya, he swallows the world and in this manner protects it.

Tiruviruttam 99

These may be simple words. But this is the good I've seen
There is only the master of knowledge
that one who took the form of a boar
lifted the world submerged in crashing waves.

Neither for the gods
who possess the great tree of wishes
nor for all the others
is there anyone else.

The verse begins with the phrase *īṉaccol* (base/low words) to describe the poem. This presents the commentators with a problem. How can the words of Nammāḻvār be considered base? Piḷḷai offers an extensive and thoughtful reading of not just this phrase, but the entire verse.

Nammāḻvār feels that to some people his words are without love, without goodness, without meaning. To these people, what he says is useless. But more importantly, these words are base because they run contrary to one's nature. After all, the burden of mokṣa should rest on Viṣṇu alone. Surrender is contiguous with one's dependence (*pāratantriya*), which is the soul's essential nature. Thus for Piḷḷai, īṉaccol evokes the core Śrīvaiṣṇava concept of *prapatti*. He goes on to explicate that people do not have the means to get rid of their sins (*pāpa*), and ignorance is the obstacle to mokṣa. But Viṣṇu is the only one with the power and the knowledge to get rid of one's transgressions. Piḷḷai also suggests that one shouldn't take īṉaccol as completely negative. Rather, there is slight irony in the statement. In this second reading, our commentator says that although only a few people may respect Nammāḻvār's words, and many will simply dismiss them as baseless, the poet still reveals them. It is like a flowering plant which produces flowers that are sometimes useful (when plucked from the tree and used in worship) and sometimes not (when they just fall to the ground).

Piḷḷai goes on to elucidate Viṣṇu's nature in relation to Nammāḻvar's identification of Varāha as the *jñāna-p-pirān̲* (master of knowledge). Piḷḷai explains that you must attach yourself to only one who has the capability to offer and give protection. Such a being is Varāha because he protected the earth (Bhūmī) without even being asked. He transformed himself and took a form contrary to his nature in order to offer protection. This avatāra thus demonstrates that Viṣṇu not only has the strength but also bears the responsibility to shelter the world. Viṣṇu has *jñāna* (knowledge), *śaktī* (power) and *prāpti* (attainment) that enable him to guard the world, and so we must attach ourselves only to him. We are his wealth and so it behoves him to care for us. Furthermore, Viṣṇu as Varāha is a refuge to people like us who are lacking, and even the gods in heaven (who may appear to have everything) seek his protection. One can become a god after performing many sacrifices, but Piḷḷai asks, why would one only desire *svarga* (heaven), when one can return from it? Shouldn't one desire a place from which one cannot return (Vaikuṇṭha)? Even the nityasūris who are always with him have need of him.

We who are mortals require his aid perhaps most of all, as we do not even know we have an *ātma* (the eternal self). We need him to prepare us as knowledge alone is insufficient. The gods, the nityasūris may have knowledge (jñāna), but this is not equal to mokṣa. In fact, jñāna can well act as an obstacle to mokṣa.

Piḷḷai is also concerned with the verse's definitive statement—*jñāna-p-pirāṉ allāl illai*—there is no one other than the master of knowledge. He cautions that this must not be taken to mean that there is nothing other than Viṣṇu. Instead, he clarifies that it means that only Viṣṇu is capable of granting mokṣa. Effort and various paths are simply obstacles to mokṣa as knowledge is unreliable, and god's intervention is the only reliable means to mokṣa. Piḷḷai's exegesis of this verse hints at what will eventually become the Teṅkalai position regarding the relationship between one's effort and Viṣṇu's grace.

APPENDIX I
INDEX OF CHARACTERS

There are four major characters in the poem—the heroine, her friend, her mother and the hero. The fortune teller makes only one brief appearance in the poem. In addition to these stock characters, familiar to us from reading Indic love poetry, the poem also has a number of verses that eschew any persona and appear to be composed in a direct address. Such verses are read purely as *svāpadeśa*, where Nammāḻvār speaks to the audience in his own voice. Although most verses can be clearly classified according to persona and voice, the *Tiruviruttam* also deliberately obliterates the demarcations between heroine/friend/mother, and a number of verses can be attributed to any of the three characters. Nonetheless, the heroine's voice dominates the poem accounting for almost half of the verses. The friend gets thirteen verses, while the mother and hero receive eleven verses each. The remaining twenty-six verses are purely svāpadeśa in content.

Persona	Verse Numbers
The heroine (*talaivi*)	3, 4, 8, 12, 13, 16, 17, 25, 27–32, 35, 36, 38–46, 48, 49, 51, 54, 56, 58, 61, 63, 70–72, 76–80, 82, 84–86
The friend (*tōḻi*)	2, 5, 7, 15, 18, 20, 22, 34, 52, 68, 69, 74, 81
The Mother (*tāy*)	19, 24, 33, 37, 47, 59, 60, 62, 73, 83, 87
The Hero (*talaivaṉ*)	6, 9–11, 14, 23, 26, 50, 55, 57, 75
The Fortune Teller (*kuṟatti*)	53
Metaphysical Verses (*svāpadeśa*). No persona, although assumed to be spoken in the voice of the heroine, who is the poet (Nammāḻvār).	1, 21, 39, 42–45, 61, 64, 79, 84–86, 88–99

APPENDIX 2

INDEX OF MOTIFS AND TYPOLOGY OF VERSES

In the *Tiruviruttam*, Nammāḻvār exploits the full range of motifs available in the corpus of Tamil love poetry. Some motifs are more common than others, and some occur in slightly different forms through the poem. Such an index allows us to chart Nammāḻvār's use of specific tropes, motifs and ideas across the poem, although these ideas may not occur in sequential verses, or indeed in verses close to each other.

As the list below indicates, evoking the night as an aeon and the relentless passage of time are two motifs that clearly dominate the poem. Indeed, the poet in his persona as the heroine indicates a certain awareness (can we call this meta-textual?) of the recurrence of the night. For example, in verse 49 she points out that she has encountered the night before, but *this* night is different. Commentators find it hard to reconcile these multiple evocations of the night, and often simply gloss the recurrence as an index of the intensification of the heroine's suffering. So, on the one hand we can read Nammāḻvār's use of the motif of the night in such a way that it becomes a character in its own right and, as I have argued in the introduction, is one horizon in the puzzle that is the *Tiruviruttam.*

Three additional motifs of central importance to the poem are: 1) the comparison of Viṣṇu's eyes/gaze with lotuses; 2) the girl's mad repetition of the names of god; and 3) swallowing, eating, consuming and devouring. Although the motif of the eyes is scattered throughout the poem, it is used in a tight sequence almost at the centre of the poem. It is one of the very few motifs that occur as a set. The second motif of the repetition of Viṣṇu's names can be set against the poet's claims of revelation and possession. In the *Tiruvirutttam*, Nammāḻvār claims only to repeat the words he has been taught by Viṣṇu. Motifs of swallowing, eating and consumption occur numerous times in the *Tiruviruttam.* It is not just Viṣṇu eating and spitting out the worlds. Clouds, the sea, the *tulasī* and even the hero participate in mutual gustatory relish.

Type of Motif/Typology	**Verse Numbers**
Kāla Mayakkam (Confusion of the Seasons)	7, 18, 52, 68, 69
Night as Aeon/without End	12, 13, 16, 36, 49, 59, 70, 72 (possibly 90, 97)
The Passage of the Night	13, 35, 40, 69, 73, 77, 80, 85, 93
The Sea	17, 18, 62, 71
The Torment of the Breeze	4, 5, 13, 27, 28, 35, 41, 47, 51, 56, 74
Messenger Verses	29, 30, 31, 32, 54, 55
Messenger Verses: Heart as the Messenger	3, 4, 46
Verses of Elopement	26, 37
Verses Addressed to the Tulasī	3–5, 12, 19, 20, 24, 25, 27, 28, 34, 35, 40, 47, 49, 51, 53, 56, 59, 70, 72, 74, 76–78, 81
Verses Referencing Swallowing, Eating and Consuming	18, 20, 21, 26, 29, 49, 56, 64, 65, 66, 71, 74, 79, 86, 91, 98

Type of Motif/Typology	Verse Numbers
Metaphysical Verses (Verses Purely in the *Svāpadeśa* Mode)	1, 21, 39, 42, 43, 44, 45, 79, 61, 64, 84–86, 88–99
The Poem as Revelation	48, 94 (possibly 99)
The Repetition of Viṣṇu's Names	20,* 48, 59, 60, 64, 71, 83, 87, 94[†]
Verses Comparing the Heroine (and Her Female Companions) to Viṣṇu's Celestial Cities and/or Its Natural Features	10, 11, 16, 23, 55, 66–68, 75
Verses Comparing Viṣṇu's Eyes to Lotuses	39, 42, 43, 45, 58,[‡] 63, 94
Direct Reference to Caṅkam Poems/Poetics	26, 55, 68

* In 20 the friend counsels the repetition of the names.

† Verses 48 and 94 are the revelation verses.

‡ In 58 he is compared to a lotus blooming in a swamp.

APPENDIX 3
INDICES OF MYTHS, PLACES AND NAMES

Myths

Narasiṁha	46
Churning the Ocean of Milk	51, 52, 57
Razing of Laṅka	36, 77, 92
Pralaya—Swallowing and Eating the Worlds	20, 56, 65, 71, 74, 79, 91
Ayan (Pinching the Head of Brahmā) and Removing Aran's Curse	86

Places

Kaṇṇan's Celestial City/ City in the Sky (Viṇṇāṭu)	9, 11, 16, 23, 57, 58
Veḥkā	26
Vēṅkaṭam/Tiruvēṅkaṭam	8, 10, 15, 31, 60, 67, 81
Tiruvaraṅkam	28
Vaikuṇṭha	30, 47, 50, 55, 66, 68, 75
Udayagiri	82

Names

Tirumāl	7, 32, 48, 52, 63, 87, 88, 95, 100
Kaṇṇan	2, 11, 12, 18, 23, 25, 26, 27, 29, 30, 37, 47, 58, 63
Beloved of Śrī and Bhū	40
Madhusūdanan	49, 59
Dāmodaran	49
Mādhavan	67
Māl	93, 97

ANNOTATIONS TO NAMMĀḺVĀR'S *TIRUVIRUTTAM*

Tiruviruttam 1

I have translated the phrase *mey niṉṟu kēṭṭu-aruḷāy* as 'stand before me embodied/graciously listen' taking some liberty with the original. *Mey* is generally translated as truth or reality, but here I have taken it in its allusive form as embodied. Partly, I have done this to connect the first verse to the penultimate one (99) in which the poet claims to have 'seen' the truth. Commentarial tradition suggests two possible ways to read *mey niṉṟu*—the first suggests that it applies to Viṣṇu as *meymaiyōṭu niṉṟu* (standing truthfully or in his natural state), and the second that it applies to the *viṇṇappam*, as in *aṭiyēṉ ceyyum mey viṇṇappam* (the truthful petition/plea of a servant).

Tiruviruttam 2

kayal: Carp (*Cyprinus fimbriatus*)

Kaṇṇaṉ: The Tamil name for Kṛṣṇa

Tiruviruttam 3

māruta breeze: A type of cool breeze

Tiruviruttam 3

The king whose fiery disc: refers to Viṣṇu's solar disc

Tiruviruttam 6

The word *kaṇṭīr* (see) which occurs in the verse's final line has been omitted and replaced in the translation with an exclamation 'O!'

Madana: Another name of Kāma, the god of love. Kama after being burned to ashes by Śiva, is born as Pradyumna, the son of Rukmiṇī and Kṛṣṇa.

Tiruviruttam 7

Tirumāl: A Tamil name for Viṣṇu

Tiruviruttam 8

Lifted the tall mountain: Refers to the myth of Kṛṣṇa lifting the Govardhana mountain to protect the cowherds from Indra's stormy wrath

Tiruviruttam 9

neytal: Indian water lily (*Nymphaea lotus alba*)

kuvaḷai: Blue water lily

The conceit is that of the neytal as the pupil, while the eye itself is the petal of the lotus. The pearl-like buds of kuvaḷai are her tears.

Tiruviruttam 10

Māyōn̲: A name of Viṣṇu that evokes his nature as a cunning, elusive trickster

Tiruvēṅkaṭam: An important sacred site in the mountains that is often used to demarcate the northern boundaries of Tamil country. It is also known by the names Tirupati and Tirumalai.

Tiruviruttam 11

Kaṇṇaṉ's celestial city: Vaikuṇṭha

keṇṭai: A freshwater fish native to Tamil country

Tiruviruttam 20

Vēlaṉ: The priest of Murukaṉ. In Caṅkam poems he is often painted as an ineffectual figure who misdiagnoses the heroine's lovesickness as possession by Murukaṉ.

Tirviruttam 21

Scoop up and eat the butter: Refers to Kṛṣṇa's childhood antics as the butter thief

Dance . . . with the humped bull: Kṛṣṇa defeats the seven bulls to win the hand of the cowherd maiden

Lovely woman of the cowherd clan: Nappiṉṉai, Kṛṣṇa's cowherd wife in the Tamil tradition

Tiruviruttam 26

Veḥkā: One of the 108 *divyadeśa*s. It is located just outside present-day Kancipuram.

Tiruviruttam 28

Tiruvaraṅkam: The sacred island-site of Srirangam in central Tamil Nadu. As one of the most important of the Tamil Vaiṣṇava sacred sites, it comes to be revered as the Bhūloka Vaikuṇṭha, Viṣṇu's celestial city on earth.

Tiruviruttam 34

'This circle destroys me': This refers to a kind of divination in Tamil country. It generally involves drawing concentric circles with an even number indicating union and an odd number predicting separation. This style of divination is used in Araiyar Cēvai, a ritual performance tradition of the Śrīvaiṣṇavas. It is called *muttukkuṟi* (divination with pearls) and is performed at Nammāḻvār's temple in Alvar Tirunagari and at Srirangam during the December Festival of Recitation. It is performed three times a year at the Āṇṭāḷ temple in Srivilliputtur—in March after the wedding festival, in August at the conclusion of the temple's Brahmotsava, and in December as part of the Mārkaḻi Nīraṭṭa Utsavam.

Tiruviruttam 35

Lord who measured the worlds: Refers to the myth of Viṣṇu as Trivikrama. In the myth, he assumes the form of a dwarf and requests three measures of land from the demon-king Bali. Growing to gargantuan proportions, he then spans the earth and the heavens in the first two strides. Having spanned all the worlds, he places the third step on the defeated king's head.

Tiruviruttam 36

Razes Laṅka's tall mansions: refers to Rāma's defeat of the ten-headed demon-king Rāvaṇa in the Rāmāyaṇa

Tiruviruttam 40

Bhū: The goddess earth, and Viṣṇu's secondary consort

Tiruviruttam 41

The lowly breeze/the cruel breeze: It torments her because of her lovesickness. In the commentary, Piḷḷai says that the breeze which was to be a sustenance and comfort to her torments her instead. She knows it from her childhood because it bothered her even at that time. He offers the analogy of a person who has lived in prison all her life and has no experience of anything different.

Tiruviruttam 45

The large boar fixed his eyes: refers to Viṣṇu's *avatāra* as Varāha, the boar, which he assumed in order to rescue the earth.

Tiruviruttam 40–45

These six verses appear almost at the poem's centre and, as befitting their special place, showcase two central themes in the *Tiruviruttam*: Viṣṇu's grace (*aruḷ*) and his eyes (*kaṇ*). The latter is figured as Viṣṇu's eyes (kaṇ) and his merciful act of glancing (*nōkku*) upon the heroine/poet. In these verses, the woman (Nammāḻvār) asks for his glance (40) and then begs for his grace (41). In the two verses that immediately follow, Viṣṇu and the heroine/poet engage in an act of mutual seeing. He sees her in 42, she returns the favour, describing the vision in an efflorescence of lotus imagery in verse 43. In verse 44, the grace of this experience is contrasted to the failure of the learned to be able to apprehend Viṣṇu, and the sequence concludes by returning once again to Viṣṇu's arresting gaze upon the heroine/poet (45).

Tiruviruttam 46

In this verse the poet alludes to the Narasiṁha avatāra. In the verse, the *asura* Hiraṇya is evoked with the epithet *poṉ-peyarōṉ*, the golden one. In the translation I have retained the epithet, instead of glossing it with the asura's name.

Tiruviruttam 51

Māya-p-pirāṉ: Lord of Māya. I have translated it here as elusive lord.

Ocean churned: Refers to Viṣṇu's *kūrma* avatāra, when he assumed the form of the tortoise to lift the sinking Mandara mountain on his back so that the gods and demons could churn the ocean to retrieve the elixir of immortality. The churning of the ocean of milk is alluded to again in *Tiruviruttam* 99.

Tiruviruttam 55

This verse alludes to a famous Caṅkam poem from the anthology *Kuṟuntokai*. In *Kuṟuntokai* 2 the hero queries the bees about the fragrance of flowers as compared to his beloved's hair.

In popular lore (as depicted in the Tamil film *Tiruviḷaiyāṭal* [1965]), this poem was composed by Śiva in response to a challenge issued by the Paṇṭiya king, who wondered if the fragrance of his queen's hair was natural. The court poet, Nakkīrar, disputed the poem's grammar, and Śiva burned (and then revived) the poet for his defiance. The story appears for the first time in Parañcōti's *Tiriviḷaiyāṭal Purāṇam*, c. sixteenth century.

The verse attributed to Iṟaiyaṉār is as follows:

He Said:
Pretty-winged bee whose livelihood is searching for pollen
    without saying [what I] desire
    Speak of what [you've] seen!
Are the flowers you know also as fragrant
    As the tresses of the young woman with close set teeth
    [and] peacock nature, in habitually united intimacy.

(*Kuṟuntokai*, trans. Eva Wilden, p. 83)

Tiruviruttam 60

The third line of this verse (*kaṭal maṇ ellām vilaiyō eṉ miḻirum kaṇ*) presents some problems, which Piḷḷai notes in his commentary. Nañcīyar reads the phrase as describing the beauty of the heroine's eyes. Bhaṭṭar responds that it is only right that it is so, for she is still a child, and her eyes are innocent with wonder. Therefore, one can see her eyes, which dart and wander observing everything, as she does not cast them down in modesty as would a young woman. Ramanujacarya in his commentary also reads it as a mark of her innocence, but says that her eyes sparkle thinking that the ocean and earth (or the earth circled by the ocean) can be bought for a price.

Tiruviruttam 64

Ṛg Veda: A collection of verses that are considered to be revealed

Tiruviruttam 68

ko<u>n</u>rai: Indian laburnum (*Cassia fistula*)

This verse also evokes a parallel to a Caṅkam poem from the Tamil anthology *Ku<u>r</u>untokai*.

What Her Girlfriend Said:

These fat cassia trees
are gullible:
    the season of the rains
    that he spoke of
    when he went through the stones
    of the desert
    is not yet here
    though these trees
    mistaking the untimely rains
    have put out
    their long arrangements of flowers
    on the twigs
    as if for a proper monsoon.

Kōvatta<u>n</u> (*Ku<u>r</u>untokai* 66, trans. A.K. Ramanujan,
in *Interior Landscape*, p. 44)

Tiruviruttam 76

āmpal: A water lily (*Nymphaea lotus*)

Tiruviruttam 78

Naraka: Refers to a demon who abducted several beautiful women and was eventually slain by Kṛṣṇa

Bāṇa: A thousand-armed demon vanquished by Kṛṣṇa. Bāṇa was a great devotee of Śiva. In the story, Kṛṣṇa's grandson Aniruddha falls in love with Bāṇa's daughter, Uṣā.

Tiruviruttam 82

A curious coincidence may be noted here with respect to the mention of the mountains of Udayagiri. The caves excavated by the Guptas in Madhya Pradesh, now known as the Udayagiri Caves, contain a famous image of Varāha (Cave 5), lifting the earth from the sea. This myth is of course of central importance to any reading of the *Tiruviruttam*.

Tiruviruttam 83

an̲ril: A bird famous for its steadfast love and attachment to its mate

Tiruviruttam 84

The second half of the verse strings together a series of epithets (*maṇiyē*: gem, *muttamē*: pearl, *māṇikkamē*: ruby). I have embellished these with adjectives to gesture to the qualities that the epithet is meant to evoke, while also seeking to evoke the lyrical quality of the same. The word 'my' (*entan̲*) occurs only once in the verse to directly qualify the verse's final line: *entan̲ maṇikkamē*, my ruby. But it may be applied to the other epithets as well.

Tiruviruttam 85

In the translation I have added the word 'precious' to qualify gem to keep it consistent with the previous verse where the same word (*maṇi*) occurs. I have added 'beloved' as an adjective to emerald. The commentators gloss the epithet *māṇikkam* (ruby) as Uttamaṉ, the excellent/perfect one, while the epithet *maragatam* (emerald) is glossed as one who ends suffering (*śramam*).

Tiruviruttam 86

Araṉ: Śiva

Ayaṉ: Brahmā

The verse makes reference to the myth of Śiva as Bhikṣāṭana. Śiva pinched off Brahmā's fifth head. As punishment, he was forced to wander the worlds carrying Brahmā's skull as a begging bowl. He wandered the worlds until he reached the city of Varanasi, where he was finally rid of the skull. In some versions of this myth, it is Viṣṇu who directs him to the sacred city.

Tiruviruttam 87

In this verse the girl is addressed in the poem as Tiru. While Tiru is taken to mean Lakṣmī, I have translated it here as 'precious', taking the secondary meaning of Tiru/Lakṣmī as wealth and prosperity. Thus, I have rendered the phrase *it-itiruviṉaiyē* (this girl whose deeds/fate is like Tiru) as 'our precious girl', to convey the intimacy of the relationship between the speaker (the mother) and the heroine. I have also added the word 'hearing' in line 3 of the translation to provide continuity.

Tiruviruttam 88

Meru: The mountain that is the cosmic axis mundi

Tiruviruttam 93

Māl: An old Tamil name for Viṣṇu

Tiruviruttam 98 and 99

I have taken some liberty and translated *īn̲accol* (base, lowly words) as 'simple words'. In English, simple evokes humility and, to some degree, a sense of self-effacement. Throughout this poem, the idea that god could be so unpretentious as to take the form of a cowherd is central. As the poem tells us repeatedly, the words are indeed simple—he stole butter—but the idea is anything but. After much experimentation I settled on simple, for it brings out all these nuances in English, in a way that base or low simply cannot.

Tiruviruttam 99

Great tree of wishes: Refers to the divine wish-fulfilling tree known as the *kalpatāru* or, as it is referred to in this verse, as *kar̲pakam*. It was one of several magical items that emerged when the gods and demons churned the ocean of milk.

Tiruviruttam 100

Kurukūr: The town identified with present-day Alvar Tirunagari in Tirunelveli, Tamil Nadu

NOTES

Entering the World of the *Tiruviruttam*

1. For an account of Nāmmāḻvār's hagiography and for issues pertaining to his date, see 'The Poet: Śaṭhakōpaṉ-Nammāḻvār', in Part II: The Measure of Time.
2. The complete title for the selection in *Hymns for the Drowning* is 'Love Poems: Four Returning Voices'. All six verses translated in this section are from the *Tiruviruttam* (7, 11, 12, 16, 60, 68). Ramanujan, *Hymns for the Drowning*, pp. 61–66.
3. Venkatesan, *The Secret Garland*, p. 160.
4. Zvelebil, *Tamil Literature*, p. 101.
5. Ramanujan and Cutler, 'From Classicism to *Bhakti*', p. 235.
6. In this story, the poems of the āḻvārs are lost and are eventually recovered by the Śrīvaiṣṇavas' first preceptor, Nāthamuni, who meditates on Nammāḻvār, seeking his assistance. Nammāḻvār answers the appeal and first reveals the *Tiruvāymoḻi* followed by the rest of his works and those of the other eleven āḻvār poets. Nāthamuni collects these songs which number around four thousand into a work that is the *Nālāyira Divya Prabandham* (The Divine Collection of Four Thousand). The Tamil Śaivas have a similar narrative of loss and recovery as it pertains to the

works of the *mūvar* Appar, Campantar and Cuntarar. However, in this story, their poems are discovered through the intervention of a Cōḻa monarch and his ministers at the great temple of Chidambaram. The poems are only partially recovered, the manuscripts having been ravaged by white ants. Thus, while the Vaiṣṇava version speaks of a complete recovery of the songs as befitting their status as revealed texts equivalent to the Vedas, the Śaiva tale is one that emphasizes nostalgia and loss and the inability to ever fully recuperate the past.

7. The twelve āḻvārs are: Poykai, Pūtam, Pēy, Tirumaḻicai, Nammāḻvār, Maturakavi, Kulaśekaraṉ, Periyāḻvār, Āṇṭaḷ, Toṇṭaraṭippoṭiāḻvār, Tiruppāṇāḻvār and Tirumaṅkai. Their works are organized as follows in the *Nālāyira Divya Prabandham*, which is divided into four books of a thousand each. The first thousand consists of the works of Periyāḻvār, Āṇṭāḷ, Kulaśekaraṉ, Tirumaḻicai, Toṇṭaratippoṭi, Tiruppāṇāḻvār, Maturakavi. The second thousand comprises three works by Tirumaṅkai. Poykai, Pēy, Pūtam, Tirumaḻicai, Nammāḻvār (three works) and the remaining poems of Tirumaṅkai are included in the third thousand. The final thousand (fourth book) is entirely the *Tiruvāymoḻi* by Nammāḻvār.
8. Ramanujan and Cutler, 'From Classicism to *Bhakti*', p. 232.
9. Narayanan, *The Way and the Goal*, p. 10.
10. Ramanujan, 'Men, Women, and Saints', p. 285.
11. Translated by Clooney and Venkatesan, *Tiruvāymoḻi*.
12. Vasudha Narayanan discusses four unique Rāmāyaṇa stories that are found in the poems of the āḻvār in *The Way and the Goal*, pp. 26–29. Another obvious example of myths associated almost exclusively with the Tamil-speaking south is that of Kṛṣṇa's cowherd consort Nappiṉṉai or Piṉṉai.
13. As A.K. Ramanujan and Norman Cutler point out in their essay 'From Classicism to *Bhakti*', the influence of akam themes and poetic sensibility on Tamil bhakti poetry has received

almost disproportionate interest. Their essay and Cutler's explication in *Songs of Experience* are important correctives in this trend. Norman Cutler traces the relationships between puṟam poetry and Tamil bhakti poetry in *Songs of Experience*, pp. 61–70. The akam themes are seen as so dominant that Friedhelm Hardy regarded loss and separation as the definitive expression of āḻvār bhakti (Hardy, *Viraha-Bhakti*). Vasudha Narayanan offers a balanced approach in *The Way and the Goal*, charting not only the Tamil influences but those of the various Sanskrit sources as well: pp. 13–14.

14. Narayanan, *The Way and the Goal*, p. 4.
15. For a further discussion of the origin and significance of the word Pāñcarātra see van Buitenen, 'Pañcarātra', pp. 291–99, and Raghavan, 'The Name Pāñcarātra', pp. 73–79.
16. I discuss the motif of revelation and possession in the section 'One Voice among Many: Revelation in the *Tiruviruttam*' in the accompanying analysis 'The Measure of Time'.
17. Translated by Carman and Narayanan in *The Tamil Veda*, p. 7.

On Reading Nammāḻvār's *Tiruviruttam*

1. Unless otherwise indicated, all translations are mine.
2. By the thirteenth century, viṇṇappam comes to encompass a wide range of ritual performative activity associated with the recitation of the *Nālāyira Divya Prabandham*, which is referred to as *viṇṇappam cey* and the reciters are known by the title *viṇṇappam ceyvār* (those who make the viṇṇappam). It appears from the inscriptional record that the term viṇṇappam ceyvār refers to the hereditary performers more commonly known as Araiyars (Leslie Orr, personal communication, 5 May 2009). In Alvar Tirunagari a family of hereditary performers known as Kavi (tracing their lineage to Maturakavi) perform a genre of songs known as Kavi Pāṭṭu as viṇṇappam, which are

rendered as part of the daily *nitya pūjā* and on the occasion of *utsavas* (festivals). The two sets of Maṇipravāḷa kavis (unique to Alvar Tirunagari) employ *śleṣa* (simultaneous narration), and are composed in praise of Viṣṇu and Nammāl̲vār.

3. I refer to the poet as Nammāl̲vār rather than as Śaṭhakōpan̲, which is the name he uses most often in his poetry. I have made this choice as it is the name by which the poet is most commonly known.
4. Friedhelm Hardy analyses the various hagiographies of Nammāl̲vār, paying particular attention to the question of caste. Of primary concern to Hardy is how a Tamil work authored by a low-caste man (Mār̲an̲ Śaṭhakōpan̲) was accepted as Veda by Maturakavi, his Brahmin student and subsequent Brahmin ācāryas (Hardy, 'The Tamil Veda of a Śūdra Saint', pp. 29–87). While Nammāl̲vār was not a Brahmin, there is nothing in his poetry that allows us to determine his caste status definitively. Given the erudition of his works, and names such as Mār̲an̲ that he assumed, it is likely that he was born into a family of some consequence.
5. The riddle refers to the relationship of the soul to the body. Maturakavi's question can be translated as: how does the embodied soul subsist? Nammāl̲vār's response is interpreted variously to mean: in an earthly body, it will subsist on food. Alternatively, it can read as: abiding in god, it (the *ātman*) will subsist on god (Carman and Narayanan, *The Tamil Veda*, p. 18).
6. This story has been adapted from the earliest recorded version in the Maṇipravāḷa *Guruparamparaprabhāvam* 6000 (c. thirteenth century). By the time the Sanskrit *Divyasūricaritam* is composed by Garuḍavāhana Paṇḍita some two centuries later, Nammāl̲vār's consequence has grown enormously. In this latter text, Nammāl̲vār plays a crucial role in Āṇṭāḷ's wedding to Viṣṇu, organizing and conducting the ceremony at Alvar Tirunagari. For further discussion of Āṇṭāḷ's story

in the *Divyasūricaritam* and Nammāḻvār's place in it, see Venkatesan, 'A Different Kind of Āṇṭāḷ Story'.

7. Nammāḻvar's return is enacted at the Annual Festival of Recitation in December at the Viṣṇu temple in Srirangam. A representative of the Śrīvaiṣṇava community recites Rāmānuja's *Śaraṇāgati Gadya* and requests the return of Nammāḻvār to earth. Viṣṇu accedes to the request (Narayanan, *Vernacular Veda*, pp. 128–29).

   Nammāḻvār's return to serve on earth echoes the Buddhist concept of the Boddhisattva, who defers his own enlightenment until all sentient beings achieve that same exalted state. Nammāḻvār's hagiography itself has clear Buddhistic elements: Nammāḻvār crawling to the tree right after birth resonates with the Buddha's first seven steps after birth, as does his meditation under the tamarind tree, which is itself evocative of the Bodhi tree. Nammāḻvār's hagiography also is suggestive of the strengthening alliance between Brahmins and agricultural castes, and one crucial to establishing the ecstatic temple-based theistic traditions of Viṣṇu and Śiva in south India.

8. The story of Nāthamuni's rediscovery of the *Tiruvāymoḻi* is recorded in the Maṇipravāḷa *Guruparamparaprabhāvam* 6000. It is Nāthamuni who is said to have first referred to this text as the Tamiḻ Veda in a short praise poem that he composed in its honour (Carman and Narayanan, *The Tamil Veda*, pp. 3–6).

9. In *Kaṇṇiṉuṇ Ciṟu Tāmpu*, Maturakavi praises Śaṭhakōpaṉ as *Kurukūr nampi* (Kurukūr's lord) in verses 1, 2, 3, 5, 6, 10 and 11, as *eṉ nampi* (my lord) in verses 4 and 9, as *deva-pirāṉ* (divine master) in verse 3 and as Kārimāṟappirāṉ (Master who is Kārimāṟaṉ) in 7 and as *em-pirāṉ* (my master) in 6.

10. The underlying assumption within traditional Śrīvaiṣṇava discourse is that the *Bhāgavata Purāṇa* is among the earliest of the Purāṇas, and predates the lives of the āḻvārs by centuries.

The so-called prophecy recorded in the *Bhāgavata Purāṇa* is as follows: 'In the beginning of Kaliyuga persons exclusively devoted to Nārāyaṇa and endowed with spiritual knowledge will be born here and there but in large numbers in the land of the Drāviḍas where flow the rivers Tāmraparṇī, Kṛtamālā (Vaigai), Payasvinī (Pālār), the holy Kāverī and the Mahānadī (Periyār) which runs westwards.' *Bhāgavata Purāṇa* XI.5, 38–40, translated by Chari, in *Philosophy and Theistic Mysticism*, pp. 11–12.

11. Govindacharya, *Holy Lives of the Azhvars*, p. 198.
12. Śrīvaiṣṇava hagiography tells us that Nāthamuni collected and compiled the āḻvār poems, which were lost and then recovered through his devotion to Nammāḻvār. While elements of the narrative are clearly exaggerated, there is no reason to question the veracity of the narrative's major contours. In that story, Nāthamuni encounters a wandering band of musicians singing a small portion of the *Tiruvāymoḻi*. Moved by the beauty of the text, he asks them to sing more only to be disappointed by their lack of knowledge. He then travels to another Vaiṣṇava *sthala*, where he is told by Parāṅkuśa Dāsaṉ, Maturakavi's disciple, to appeal to Nammāḻvār by reciting Maturakavi's text. Eventually, Nammāḻvār appears before him, and reveals not only the *Tiruvāymoḻi* but the entire corpus of the *Divya Prabandham*. It is quite likely that the āḻvār songs were, if not lost, at least not in active circulation. Given the stress on performance in the poems themselves, it is equally possible that the poems were transmitted by bands of wandering musicians. As N. Jagadeesan points out, the Śrīvaiṣṇava saṁpradāyas seem to have been concerned with establishing neat lines of succession, which the above story takes great pains to demonstrate. Nāthamuni is enfolded into the direct line of lineal descent through Parāṅkuśa Dāsaṉ who was Maturakavi's student. But the hagiography also tells us that Nāthamuni is a direct disciple of Nammāḻvār as he receives

the text(s) directly from the āḻvār (Jagadeesan, *History of Sri Vaishnavism in the Tamil Country*, p. 41). See the discussion of aṁśa theory in relation to Āṇṭāḷ in Venkatesan, *Āṇṭāḷ and Her Magic Mirror*. The process of canonization, particularly that of the *Tiruvāymoḻi* as Drāviḍa Veda, was no doubt an important step in canonizing the āḻvārs as a whole. This process went hand in hand with the careful production of commentaries beginning with Nammāḻvār's magnum opus. For a succinct discussion of the *Tiruvāymoḻi* as the Tamiḻ Veda see Carman and Narayanan, *The Tamil Veda*, pp. 4–7.

13. Hardy, *Viraha-Bhakti*, pp. 267–68. Vedānta Deśika provides a list in his *Prabandhasāram*, which differs from the one in the *Rāmānuja Nūṟṟantāti*. Krishnaswami Aiyankar points out that the order of Vedānta Deśika's list of āḻvārs must replicate contemporary chronology, one that is reflected in the *Guruparamparaprābhavams* (the major Śrīvaiṣṇava hagiographies) that were already in circulation (Aiyangar, *Early History of Vaishnavism*, pp. 37–41).
14. The *Rāmānuja Nūṟṟantāti* 7 provides the list, which is as follows: Poykai, Pūtam, Pēy, Tiruppaṉāḻvār, Tirumaḻicai, Toṇṭaraṭippoṭi, Kulaśekara, Periyāḻvār, Āṇṭāḷ, Tirumaṅkai.
15. Zvelebil, *Tamil Literature*, p. 153.
16. Hardy offers a typically comprehensive survey of the question of dating Nammāḻvār (Hardy, *Viraha-Bhakti*, pp. 261–69).
17. Rao, *Sir Subrahmanya Ayyar Lectures*, p. 18. Gopinatha Rao describes finding the two stone inscriptions—one in Tamil and the other in Sanskrit—at Anamalai in 1906.
18. Ibid., pp. 18–21. Rao also uses the astronomical data of the *Guruparamparaprabhāvams* to yield a date of 798 CE for Nammāḻvār's birth.
19. Sastri, *A History of South India*, p. 172.
20. Pillai, *History of Tamil Language*, pp. 129–31.
21. Ibid., p. 132.
22. Aiyangar, *Early History of Vaishnavism*, pp. 53–55.

23. Ibid., p. 84, fn. 1. Here, Aiyangar produces *Tiruviruttam* 94 as evidence in support of this claim.
24. Ramanujam, *History of Vaishnavism*, pp. 239–41.
25. Ibid., p. 242.
26. Nagaswamy, 'A New Pandya Record and the Dates of Nayanmars and Alvars'.
27. Hardy, *Viraha-Bhakti*, pp. 308–09.
28. Zvelebil, *Tamil Literature*, p. 161.
29. Some editions of the *Nālāyira Divya Prabandham* list the Iyarpā as constituting the third thousand of the text, with the 1100 verses of the *Tiruvāymoli* as the final book. In other editions, the order is switched, and the *Tiruvāymoli* makes up the third thousand, while the Iyarpā acts as the collection's conclusion. Regardless of where the Iyarpā is placed, the *Tiruviruttam* always follows the four compositions of the first four ālvār, and precedes Nammālvār's remaining two compositions, the *Tiruvāciriyam* (seven verses) and *Periya Tiruvantāti* (eighty-seven verses).
30. Hardy divides the *Divya Prabandham* into three kinds of poetic material. The first group is constituted of antātis in *veṇpā* metre, the second is the *Tirumoli*, which contains emotional material, and the third division is made up of experimental poems. Although the *Tiruviruttam* replaces the veṇpā with the *viruttam* metre, he still regards it a conventional work experimenting with *akattiṇai* themes (Hardy, *Viraha-Bhakti*, pp. 270–71).
31. Appar also composes a poem called the *Tiruviruttam* (*Appar Tēvāram*, 4.80–4.113), named on account of its use of the viruttam metre. In the *Tēvāram* it is also referred to as *kattaḷaikkalitturai*. Many of the verses from Appar's *Tiruviruttam* have been lost. The Vaiṣṇava and Śaiva *Tiruviruttams* have little in common in terms of content. Appar's poem is not a love poem. But as bhakti poems, both works share an ethos of rich imagery, thick descriptions (4.80 is an extravagant

foot-to-head description of a dancing Śiva) and desperate longing for divine grace. For a detailed discussion of the use of viruttam in the *Tēvāram* see Peterson, *Poems to Śiva*, pp. 61–67.

32. Peterson, *Poems to Śiva*, pp. 64–67.
33. One can map the entire *Tiruviruttam* in this fashion, noting the ways in which the antāti indexes shifts in ideas, tones or themes.
34. Nammāḻvār uses the word *mey* (truth, reality, soul) to describe Viṣṇu's form. But the use of mey in the phrase *mey niṉṟu kēṭṭu-aruḷāy* is ambiguous. In my translation, I have read it allusively. Partly I have done this to connect the first verse to the penultimate one (99) in which the poet claims to have 'seen' the truth. Commentarial tradition suggests two possible ways to read mey niṉṟu . . . The first suggests taking it as applying to Viṣṇu as *meymaiyōṭu niṉṟu* (standing truthfully or in his natural state). The second reads mey with viṇṇappam, as in *aṭiyēṉ ceyyum mey viṇṇappam* (the truthful petition/plea made by a servant). Given the stress the *Tiruviruttam* places on seeing and enjoying god in an embodied form—the poem is full of lush, extravagant descriptions of Viṣṇu's eyes, the colour of his form and his many attributes—it is not so far-fetched that a desire for a vision of an embodied divinity is reflected in the poem's opening lines.
35. Carman and Narayanan ask us to take seriously the claims Nammāḻvār makes about physical union with Viṣṇu. A careful and sustained reading of the metaphor of swallowing in the *Tiruvāymoḻi* leads them to conclude that 'God's inclusion and pervasion of the universe and the poet is then the fundamental and final reality; and this union is experienced by Nammāḻvar in the flesh, with full-blooded passion' (Carman and Narayanan, *The Tamil Veda*, p. 179).
36. A paraphrase of Periyavāccāṉ Piḷḷai's commentary for *Tiruviruttam* 20 can be found in Part III.

37. Clooney and Venkatesan (trans.), *Tiruvāymoḻi*.
38. Piḷḷai, *Tiruviruttam Vyākhyāṉam*, p. 21.
39. Ibid., pp. 53–56.
40. Takahashi, *Poetry and Poetics*, pp. 71–72.
41. Piḷḷai, *Tiruviruttam Vyākhyāṉam*, pp. 53–56.
42. Ibid., p. 56.
43. *Songs of Experience* (Norman Cutler), and the seminal, jointly authored paper by A.K. Ramanujan and Norman Cutler, 'From Classicism to *Bhakti*', map the specific transformations between the two poetic traditions. Indira Peterson's *Poems to Śiva* analyses the Śaiva *Tēvāram* poets' debt to the antecedent literary tradition, while Friedhelm Hardy does the same for the āḻvār poets in *Viraha-Bhakti*.
44. See *Tiruvāymoḻi* X.3.5 for an excellent example of Nammāḻvār's handling of Caṅkam themes, or even *Tiruviruttam* 68 for a deft reworking of a famous Caṅkam poem. The latter example has been discussed by A.K. Ramanujan in his essay 'Where Mirrors Are Windows'.
45. Parthasarathy (trans.), *The Tale of an Anklet*. p. 111.
46. Takahashi, *Poetry and Poetics*, p. 63. Martha Selby discusses the significance of the middle placement of pālai in the usual listing of the *aintiṇai* (five landscapes). See Selby, 'Dialogues of Space, Desire, and Gender', p. 26.
47. For a discussion of how the commentator Periyavāccāṉ Piḷḷai handles this verse, see Venkatesan, 'Double the Pleasure'.
48. Selby, *Tamil Love Poetry*, p. 13.
49. For example, you may have a patikam on Tillai in *Appar Tēvāram* V.1 or a *tirumoḻi* on the salvific potential of the sacred name Nārāyaṇa (*Periya Tirumoḻi* I.1) by Tirumaṅkai.
50. Selby, *Tamil Love Poetry*, p. 13. One could map the *Tiruviruttam* in a similar fashion, beginning with the verses of lament and distress that end in the comforting promise of perpetual union with Viṣṇu.

51. Takahashi points out that the consensus of modern scholars is that 'the schematic treatment of solitary situations as a narrative sequence' originated in *Iṟaiyaṉār Akapporuḷ* and reached completion in the kōvais (Takahashi, *Poetry and Poetics*, p. 256).
52. Ibid., p. 38.
53. Hardy, *Viraha-Bhakti*, pp. 324–25. Hardy suggests that the *Tiruviruttam* was the inspiration for the *Tirukkōvaiyār* because of the similar manner in which Śiva and Viṣṇu function in the two poems. That is, in the way the *Tiruviruttam*'s entire emotional content refers to Viṣṇu (as the *karu*), the *Tirukkōvaiyār* is moulded such that its emotional referent is Śiva.
54. Vaiyapuri Pillai points to linguistic similarities between the *Tiruvācakam* and *Tiruvāymoḻi*, particularly in regard to the titles of the respective texts. He also sees the *Tiruviruttam* and *Tirukkōvaiyār* as a pair (Pillai, *History of Tamil Language*, p. 132).
55. Cutler, 'Four Spatial Realms in *Tirukkōvaiyār*', p. 55. Depending on whether you date Nammāḻvār to the late eighth or early to mid ninth century, the two poets were separated by around fifty to seventy-five years.
56. Takahashi, *Poetry and Poetics*, pp. 39–40.
57. Venugopal charts and identifies ten kiḷavi verses for the *Tiruviruttam* (Venugopal, *Tiruvirttamum Tirukkōvaiyārum*, pp. 62–64).
58. Hardy, *Viraha-Bhakti*, p. 320.
59. Verses 25, 54 and 80 refer to Viṣṇu as king (*kōṉ*). She refers to him as master in verse 1 (talaivā, leader), 50 (*nāyakaṉ*, hero), 53 (*talaimakaṉ*, head), 59 (*nāṭaṉ*, lord of the place, *nāṭu*), 61 (nāyakaṉ), 77 (*pirāṉ*, lord), 79 (nātaṉ). It is worth noting that the poet deliberately uses words that invoke both a heroic and poetic/dramatic persona: talaivā, nāyakaṉ, talaimakaṉ and nāṭaṉ is the case in point.

60. Verses 5, 25 and 33 refer to the bending of the Viṣṇu's sceptre on account of his injustice towards the girl.
61. A word like 'master' is often used in both akam and puṟam contexts. In both cases it evokes the protective, sheltering quality shared by the anonymous hero of the akam poems and the king of the puṟam world. Martha Selby illustrates the complementarity of akam and puṟam as it coalesces around a figure like the akam hero or the puṟam king. See Selby, 'Dialogues of Space, Desire, and Gender', pp. 21–24.
62. In *Viraha-Bhakti*, Friedhelm Hardy provides a close reading of the symbolic system of the *Tiruviruttam* through the lens of Caṅkam poetry. Even as he says that the 'emotional relationship between the (poetic) man and woman . . . is made the content of the Āḻvār's "communication"' (p. 320), he is quick to assert that the hero and heroine do not refer to either Viṣṇu or the āḻvār. To do so would destroy the poem's poetic structure (p. 324). I would argue that the poem functions by encouraging the reader to oscillate between the two poles of persona and poet, that the poem's many meanings are produced through the dialectical relationships engendered by bringing its multiple, concentric layers into dialogue.
63. Cutler, *Songs of Experience*, p. 93. The dual 'allegorical' meaning is similar to the Śrīvaiṣṇava interpretation of the text along the lines of anyāpadeśa and svāpadeśa.
64. The legend of the composition of the *Tirukkōvaiyār* places Śiva in the role of both patron and audience. The story is recorded in the *Tiruvātuvūr Purāṇam*, a fifteenth-century Tamil hagiography about Māṇikkavācakar. Śiva appears before Māṇikkavācakar and asks him to compose a kōvai. The poet does so and the god writes it down. Then Śiva disappears, only to reappear and sing the kōvai to his gathered devotees. David Shulman provides a detailed analysis of this narrative in '*Tirukkovaiyār:* Downstream into God', pp. 135–39.

65. Cutler, *Songs of Experience*, p. 153.
66. Shulman, '*Tirukkovaiyār:* Downstream into God', p. 139.
67. Ibid., pp. 139–41.
68. Vasu Renganathan provides a comprehensive survey of similes used in Caṅkam poetry in an unpublished paper, 'The Element of Beauty and the Use of Similes in Tamil Poetics'. I wish to thank him for sharing his work with me. A.K. Ramanujan's essay 'Towards an Anthology of City Images' also provides a useful typological model on the descriptions of cities in Sanskrit and Tamil literary texts.
69. Cutler, *Songs of Experience*, p. 158.
70. Cutler, 'Four Spatial Realms in *Tirukkōvaiyār*', p. 49.
71. Trawick, 'Ambiguity in the Oral Exegesis of a Sacred Text', p. 316.
72. See Venkatesan, *The Secret Garland* for a detailed discussion of space in the *Tiruppāvai* and *Nācciyār Tirumoḻi*.
73. Damodaran, *Ācārya Hṛdayam: A Critical Study*, pp. 1–2.
74. He is equally concerned with the poems' symbolism drawing elaborate concordances for flowers, bees, birds, insects and characters. Some of these symbolic associations are familiar—the *haṁsa* bird's ability to separate milk from water—while others may be more specific to the Śrīvaiṣṇava traditions—the peacocks' call as the sound of Viṣṇu's name. See G. Damodaran's careful explication and charts for the various concordances (*Ācārya Hṛdayam: A Critical Study*, pp. 58–82).
75. See Nāyaṉār, *Ācārya Hṛdayam*, pp. 93–95. Also see Damodaran, *Ācārya Hṛdayam: A Critical Study* for a detailed discussion of the text. Chapter 5 (pp. 58–82) provides an exhaustive discussion of the *Ācārya Hṛdayam*'s explication of Nammāḻvār's female characters.
76. Hopkins, '"I Walk Weeping in Pangs of a Mother's Torment for Her Children"', p. 53.
77. Pandian, *Crooked Stalks*, p. 216.

78. Both Isabelle Clark-Decès and Anand Pandian in their analyses of oppu point out the significance of the comparative element in Tamil lament songs, although they differ in their interpretation of *what* such comparisons are meant to achieve.
79. Tamil laments generally fall under the broad category of folk songs performed by women of the lower castes during funerals. They are part of a large complex of Tamil mortuary rituals, during which women gather to vent and lament together. Isabelle Clark-Decès's superb anthropological study of Tamil crying songs finds the concept of kuṟai, or lack/ inadequacy, the fundamental building block of the oppu. That is, women lament not for the dead or their kin, but for themselves: using the particular instance of death to speak of the ideal, of the general. *This* is kuṟai, a lack, a gap, the sense of being left behind. The greater the kuṟai, the more plaintive is the lament. And greater the sense of disquiet, the more affective is the lament. Both lack and disquiet—kuṟai and *aṅkalāyppu*—are predicated on comparison and evaluation. But despite all these rhetorical gestures towards sympathy, Clark-Decès sees women's laments primarily as an individual expression, although these voices may dissolve into a 'de-centered collage of voices' (Clark-Decès, *No One Cries for the Dead*, p. 9). Anand Pandian, in contrast, sees the oppu as living up to its name. For him, it is not so much kuṟai or aṅkalāyppu that makes for an effective lament. It is the nature of the self itself, what he terms the '*aqueous* self'. Thus, within the framework of the aqueous self, of the *iramāṉa maṉam*, the lament obliterates the 'boundaries between self and other; between self and landscape, and ultimately between past and present' (Pandian, *Crooked Stalks*, p. 208).
80. Hopkins, '"I Walk Weeping in Pangs of a Mother's Torment for Her Children"', p. 75.
81. The exact phrase in this verse is *eṉ colli pulampuvaṉē*, which in a literal translation would read as 'what can I say and lament?'.

82. In the *Tiruviruttam*, the hero too offers up some laments. Two striking verses that invoke water imagery and unbound emotion are *Tiruviruttam* 50 and 57. In both of these verses, particularly in 57, the hero is subject to those unruly, undammed emotions that one often attributes to the heroine. As he says in a rare kind of confessional, 'I am like the ocean with its crashing waves / giving up its nectar / when Kaṇṇan churned it with his mountain.' In many of the hero verses, it is the heroine who is described as brimming with an overflow of emotion: her eyes darting like fish, her tears spilling from eyes like pearls. It is this overflow of emotion that slays him and attracts him (*Tiruviruttam* 9). This is the wealth that he treasures (*Tiruviruttam* 11).
83. Patton and Hawley, introduction to *Holy Tears*, p. 1.
84. This *aqueous* maṉam, in Tamil, the īramānā maṉam (literally, moist/wet heart-mind) is always set in opposition to the stone-hearted one (*kal-maṉacu*). One heart is fluid, malleable, unbound, while the other is rigid, bound and incapable of transformation. It is this properly aqueous self that can cultivate sympathy as a virtue (Pandian, *Crooked Stalks*, pp. 181–83).
85. Shulman, 'Embracing the Subject', p. 83.
86. Hardy, *Viraha-Bhakti*, p. 317.
87. Clooney, '"I Created Land and Sea"', p. 244.
88. Ibid., pp. 239–41.
89. Ibid., pp. 242–44.
90. Ibid., p. 247.
91. Clooney and Venkatesan (trans.), *Tiruvāymoḻi*.
92. This phrase *eṉ colli niṟpaṉ* (what can I say?) is the antāti that links VII.9.1 and VII.9.2, drawing attention to its significance. The content of intermingling speech and speakers in VII.9.2 is set between these two speech acts: the poet's apparent speechlessness (eṉ colli niṟpaṉ) and god's speech (*eṉ muṉ collum*—he who speaks before me).

In Piḷḷai's interpretation of this decad (VII.9), the verses are born from the joy the poet experiences from his union with Viṣṇu, during which he speaks through him. In the commentary for this verse, Piḷḷai tells us that Viṣṇu makes Nammāḻvār his instrument to sing the *Tiruvāymoḻi* in the same way that he is the soul of the other deities through whom he manages the creation and destruction of the world. John Carman and Vasudha Narayanan provide the commentary for all eleven verses in this decad (*The Tamil Veda*, pp. 234–38).

93. Shulman, 'Embracing the Subject', pp. 86–87.
94. Clooney, '"I Created Land and Sea"', pp. 239–40.
95. Nabokov, *Religion against the Self*, pp. 31–32.
96. Carman and Narayanan, *The Tamil Veda*, pp. 165–75.
97. For example, *Tiruviruttam* 20 refers to the swallowing of the worlds, 21 to butter eating (both of which are the first instances that the particular myth is alluded to in the poem). In the verses of the 50s set of the *Tiruviruttam*, all three myths appear in approximate closeness. Verses 51 and 52 allude to the churning of the ocean, 54 to the stealing of butter and 56 to the swallowing of the worlds. There is only one time when two of these myths occur together. This is in *Tiruviruttam* 91 where the *pralaya* myth and butter eating are juxtaposed. See Appendix 3 for the Index of Myths in the *Tiruviruttam*.
98. This is an apt phrase that Frank Clooney uses to describe the god-consciousness experienced by the girl in *Tiruvāymoḻi* V.6 (Clooney, '"I Created Land and Sea"', pp. 239–40).
99. Clooney, *Seeing through Texts*.
100. Friedhelm Hardy and A.K. Ramanujan are the best representatives of this position, seeing commentarial interventions as technical and scholastic. Francis Clooney provides a nuanced corrective to this position through a careful and considered reading of decads from the *Tiruvāymoḻi*. See Clooney, '"I Created Land and Sea"' and 'Nammāḻvār's

Glorious Tiruvallavāḻ' for two important case studies. My readings and approach to Śrīvaiṣṇava commentary owe much to Frank Clooney's early work.

101. Frank Clooney analyses the use of Sanskrit scriptural sources in the commentaries on the *Tiruvāymoḻi* in 'Nammāḻvār's Glorious Tiruvallavāḻ'. My concern is primarily with the commentators' use of Tamil āḻvār sources.
102. The *Ācārya Hṛdayam* is mainly concerned with Nammāḻvār (*Tiruvāymoḻi*), although the works of the other āḻvār are also quoted. This creates the impression that the āḻvār speak with one voice, but that voice(s) is subsumed into that of Nammāḻvār's. In a traditional metaphor, Nammāḻvār is seen as the body (Vedas) and the works of the other āḻvār are the limbs (Vedāṅgas). See Damodaran, *Ācārya Hṛdayam: A Critical Study*, p. 1.
103. Ramanujan, 'Afterword', *Hymns for the Drowning*, p. 151.
104. Shulman, '*Tirukkovaiyār*: Downstream into God', p. 133.
105. Their very names evoke notions of fluidity and disembodiment. Poykai's name means pond, Pēy means ghost, and Pūtam is a ghoul.
106. Vasudha Narayanan uses the meeting of the first three āḻvār and their resulting poems as a metaphor for the spreading of bhakti in Tamil country (Narayanan, '"With the Earth as a Lamp and the Sun as the Flame": Lighting Devotion in South India').
107. Cutler, *Songs of Experience*, p. 125.
108. Ibid., p. 127.
109. Ibid., p. 130.
110. For a discussion of the Śrīvaiṣṇava concept of anubhava see Hopkins, *Singing the Body of God* and 'Extravagant Beholding', and Venkatesan, *The Secret Garland*, pp. 31–33.
111. This is the succinct situational summation presented by Piḷḷai for *Tiruviruttam* 68.

112. The division of the commentarial section is adapted from Venkatesan, 'Double the Pleasure'. Francis Clooney also provides a step-by-step anatomy of a commentary in his 'Nammāḻvār's Glorious Tiruvallavāḻ'.
113. Piḷḷai, *Tiruviruttam Vyākhyāṉam*, pp. 160–61.
114. I offer paraphrases of Periyavāccāṉ Piḷḷai's commentary to six verses from the *Tiruviruttam*. These can be found in Part III.
115. A.K. Ramanujan discusses *Tiruviruttam* 68 and its Caṅkam parallel to *Kuṟuntokai* 66 in his article 'Where Mirrors Are Windows'.
116. Piḷḷai, *Tiruviruttam Vyākhyāṉam*, pp. 357–59.
117. Selby, *Tamil Love Poetry*, p. 14.
118. Ibid., p. 13.
119. J.S.M. Hooper graduated from Oxford University (Corpus Christi College) with an MA. In his preface to *Bible Translation in India, Pakistan and Ceylon* (1938) he indicates that he arrived in India in 1905. He served as the principal of Wesley College of Madras, a fact he notes in the title page of *Hymns of the Ālvārs*. He was active in Christian missionary societies, appointed to the General Committee of the Indian Literature Fund founded in 1920. Hooper was involved in other ways as well, serving as the general secretary in India of the British and Foreign Bible Society (*Proceedings of the 5th Meeting of the National Christian Council, Nagpur*, 31 December 1932–4 January 1933, p. 31). By 1946, he was well known for having established the Bible Society of India and Ceylon, an achievement noted in the *Proceedings of the 10th Annual Meeting of the National Christian Council, Nagpur*, p. 41. He was also instrumental in steering the Church Union Movement along with Dr J.J. Banninga (1875–1963) from 1920 until 1947 through a series of negotiations that eventually led to the formation of the Church of South India (Newbigin, *The Reunion of the Church*, p. 1). Towards this end, Hooper also worked closely with Lesslie Newbigin (1909–1998) in

his capacity as the British Methodist Secretary of the Joint Committee of the Church union in south India (Wainwright, *Lesslie Newbigin: A Theological Life*, p. 85). Between 1934 and 1947, J.S.M. Hooper served as the editor of a quarterly, *Church Union News and Views*, which was founded in 1930. This quarterly was an important vehicle that published articles by Indian Christians and British missionaries on the move towards Church union. In addition, Hooper and his co-editor J.J. Banninga (editor, 1930–33) published several editorials on the history of the negotiations towards Church union (Sundkler, *Church of South India*, p. 201). Furthermore, Hooper worked closely with Newbigin and Bishop V.S. Azariah (1874–1945), two important figures in the move towards Church union, in drafting the Service of Inauguration that would take place on 27 September 1947 at St George's Cathedral, Madras (Wainwright, op. cit., p. 272). Given his crucial role as 'pilot of South Indian Union' as Sundkler characterized it (op. cit., p. 339), it is no surprise that this Convener of the Joint Committee of the union was honoured for his role in the unification by being invited to deliver the inaugural sermon at St George's Cathedral in Madras on 27 September 1947, an event attended by close to 3000 people (Graham, 'The Inauguration of the Church of South India', pp. 50–51). Even after ecclesiastical union was achieved in 1947, Hooper continued to wield considerable power in his capacity as the Convener of the Continuation Committee as the Church of South India moved towards administrative union (Sundkler, op. cit., p. 344). Hooper was the author of several works, including what appears to be his first work, *The Approach to the Gospel* (SCM Press, 1910). This was followed by *Hymns of the Ālvārs* and *The Bible in India with a Chapter on Ceylon*.

120. The Heritage of India Series began in 1915. The first publication was K.J. Saunders's *The Heart of Buddhism*.

Between 1915 and 1923, the year of Farquhar's departure from India, sixteen books on a wide range of topics were published under its banner. These included works on Indian painting (1918), the songs of the Maratha poets (1920), verses from the *Ṛg Veda* (1922), on Indian coins (1922), poems by Indian women (1923) and on classical Sanskrit literature (1923). See Sharpe, *Not to Destroy But to Fulfil*, p. 380.

121. J.N. Farquhar, quoted in Sharpe, *Not to Destroy but to Fulfil*, p. 308.
122. 'Editorial Preface' to Kingsbury and Phillips, *Hymns of the Tamil Śaivite Saints*. No page number.
123. Ibid.
124. Sharpe, *Not to Destroy but to Fulfil*, p. 380.
125. Sundkler, *Church of South India*, p. 134.
126. J.N. Farquhar quoted in Sharpe, *Not to Destroy but to Fulfil*, p. 305.
127. Ibid.
128. *Proceedings of the 5th Meeting of the National Christian Council, Nagpur*, p. vii.
129. Sharpe, *Not to Destroy but to Fulfil*, pp. 304–05. F. Kingsbury, who was also involved in the Church Union Movement, was suspended from the ministry in 1926 for making statements that were seen as contrary to Church orthodoxy. It took several years before he was reinstated (Sundkler, *Church of South India*, p. 173).
130. Hooper, preface to *Hymns of the Ālvārs*. Farquhar died on 17 July 1929. *Hymns of the Ālvārs* must have been published in early 1929 for Hooper does not mention Dr Farquhar's passing in his preface or introduction. His acknowledgement of Farquhar's contribution in the preface gives every impression that Farquhar was still alive at the time of publication. By 1921 Hooper had certainly already been commissioned to undertake the translation of the āḻvār poets, and the title is listed as a forthcoming/proposed work under the category

of 'Vernacular Literature' in Kingsbury and Phillips, *Hymns of the Tamil Śaivite Saints*, p. ii.

131. Richards, review of *The Heritage of India Series: Hymns of the Ālvārs* by J.S.M. Hooper, p. 591.
132. Hooper appears to rely mainly on Farquhar's dating. See, for instance, his discussion of the dating of the *Bhāgavata Purāṇa* in introduction to *Hymns of the Ālvārs*, pp. 18–19.
133. Hooper, *Hymns of the Ālvārs*, pp. 19–20. In all of this, Hooper's translation follows the pattern of Kingsbury and Phillips's *Hymns of the Tamil Śaivite Saints*. Here too the two translators provide bronze images of the four saints translated (Appar, Campantar, Cuntarar and Māṇikkavācakar), while cautioning the reader that the images are not portraits but imaginative renderings for worship. Hooper's offering does pale in comparison to the work produced by Kingsbury and Phillips. Although their introduction is brief and their translation not that much better than Hooper's, they are attentive to issues of iconography and the symbolism of the major Śaiva myths. The difference in quality may well have to do with the already established tradition of scholarship on Tamil Śaivism, reaching a zenith in G.U. Pope's English translation of Māṇikkavācakar's *Tiruvācakam* (1900). Tamil Vaiṣṇavism in comparison had suffered. Hooper's English translation of selections from the *Divya Prabandham* may well have been the first such effort.
134. Hardy, *Viraha-Bhakti*, p. 318.
135. See Clooney, *Seeing through Texts*, and Carman and Narayanan, *The Tamil Veda*, for theoretically interesting ways of reclaiming the Śrīvaiṣṇava commentarial traditions.
136. Hooper, *Hymns of the Ālvārs*, p. 60.
137. Hooper, preface to *Hymns of the Ālvārs*, p. i.
138. Hardy suggests that Hooper simply avoids those verses that are overtly erotic. A careful survey of the translation does not support this conclusion (Hardy, *Viraha-Bhakti*, pp. 318–19).

139. Hooper, *Hymns of the Ālvārs*, p. 58.
140. Ibid., p. 59.
141. Ibid., p. 61.
142. Nandakumar, *Nammāḻvār's 'Tiruviruttam'*, p. 32.
143. Ibid., p. 17.
144. Ramanujan, introduction to *Hymns for the Drowning*, p. xv.
145. Ramanujan, 'Where Mirrors Are Windows'. Also see Ramanujan, 'Is There an Indian Way of Thinking?' for further discussion on similar issues.
146. Ramanujan, *Hymns for the Drowning*, p. 63.
147. Bharati, *The Sacred Book of Four Thousand*, p. 699.
148. The two major ritual traditions at the Alvar Tirunagari temple associated with Nammāḻvār's poetry are the Araiyar Cēvai and the Kavi Pāṭṭu. Araiyar Cēvai takes its most elaborate form during the Annual Festival of Recitation (*Adhyāyanotsavam*) that occurs over the course of twenty days in the month of Mārkaḻi (mid-December to mid-January). Today, the Cēvai is performed by Brahmin men, who are hereditary performers, at the temples of Srirangam, Srivilliputtur and Alvar Tirunagari. Nammāḻvār's *Tiruvāymoḻi* is recited and interpreted over the course of the second half of the festival known as Irā-Pāṭṭu at all three temples, while the *Tiruviruttam* is performed during the first ten days known as Pakal Pāṭṭu. The second performance tradition is known as Kavi Pāṭṭu. It too is performed by a family of Brahmin men who claim descent from Maturakavi. The Kavi Pāṭṭu repertoire is unique to Alvar Tirunagari. It consists of sets of Maṇipravāḷa śleṣa prose poems that are known as 'Perumāḷ Kavi', 'Āḻvār Kavi' and 'Ti<u>n</u>appaṭi Kavi'. Lines from the *Tiruviruttam* are interwoven into these kavis, with particular emphasis placed on the line jñāna-p-pirā<u>n</u> allāl illai (there is no one but the master of knowledge) from *Tiruviruttam* 99. This kavi is performed before the Nammāḻvār *sannidhi* as part

of the morning *nitya utsavam* at the Alvar Tirunagari temple. The kavis are also referred to as viṇṇappam (petition). See Venkatesan, 'The Poet's Song' (forthcoming).

149. See Appendix 2 (Index of Motifs) for a list of *Tiruviruttam* verses that focus on Viṣṇu's eyes.

GLOSSARY

Words are marked with * *to indicate a cross-reference*

Adhyayanotsavam: The Annual Festival of Recitation that takes place in the Tamil month of Mārkaḻi*

Aiṅkuṟunūṟu: A classical Tamil anthology of five hundred short love poems dated to the third century

Akam: Literally, interior/inner. It refers to the category of Tamil classical poems that deal with love and domestic affairs.

Akapporuḷ: Poems which contain *akam* content

Alaṅkāra: Ornamentation, decoration

Aṁśa: An emanation of Viṣṇu

Antāti: a poetic form where the end syllables or words of a verse are repeated as the first syllables or words of the verse that immediately follows it

Aṉṟil: A bird that is often used in Tamil love poetry to evoke steadfastness

Anubhava: Enjoyment

Anubhava grantha: A text of enjoyment. Śrīvaiṣṇavas* use it to refer to commentary.

Anyāpadeśa: The outer or exoteric meaning of a text

Araiyar Cēvai: A hereditary ritual tradition associated with the *Nālāyira Divya Prabandham**

Araṉ: Śiva

Aruḷ: Grace, mercy, compassion

Asura: The natural enemies of the gods (*sura*), often translated into English as demons

Avatāra: Descent. Refers to the ten descents/interventions of Viṣṇu

Ayaṉ: Brahmā

Ācārya: Teacher

Ācārya Hṛdayam: Literally, the heart of the teacher. A Maṇipravāḷa synthesis of the meaning of the *Tiruvāymoḻi**

Āḻvār: Literally, the one who drowns, one who is immersed, coming from the Tamil root *āḻ*—to drown/to be immersed. The twelve poet-saints of the Śrīvaiṣṇava tradition whose compositions comprise the *Nālāyira Divya Prabandham**

Āmpal: A water lily

Āṇṭāḷ: The sole female *āḻvār** poet. She authored two poems, the *Tiruppāvai** and the *Nācciyār Tirumoḻi**

Ātman: The eternal undying self

Bāṇa: A thousand-armed *asura** and devotee of Śiva who was vanquished by Kṛṣṇa

Bhāgavatas: Devotees of Viṣṇu

Bhāgavata Purāṇa: One of the most important Purāṇas extolling the virtues of Viṣṇu. It contains eighteen books. The tenth book, which is the longest, is concerned with Kṛṣṇa's exploits.

Bhū: The goddess earth. She is considered Viṣṇu's secondary consort.

Caṅkam: Literally, academy. It refers to the corpus of Tamil literary works composed between the first and third centuries CE.

Cilappatikāram: A Jain Tamil epic composed by Ilaṅkō Aṭikaḷ dated to between the fifth and sixth centuries CE

Ci<u>rr</u>i<u>n</u>pam: Worldly pleasures

Cūrṇikai: Sutra, short aphoristic statement. Refers to the individual verses from the *Ācārya Hṛdayam**

Devagā<u>n</u>am: Divine music. Refers to Srirama Bharati's reimagined Araiyar Cēvai

Divyasūricaritam: A fifteenth-century Sanskrit hagiography of the Śrīvaiṣṇava ā<u>l</u>vār* and *ācārya**

Gopī: Cowherd maidens

Guruparamparaprabhāvam: Maṇipravāḷa* hagiographies of the Śrīvaiṣṇava ā<u>l</u>vār* and ācārya.* There are two major versions of the text known as the 6000 and 3000.

Kṛṣṇa: The ninth *avatāra** of Viṣṇu

Iya<u>r</u>pā: A section of the *Nālāyira Divya Prabandham** that contains many of the experimental works

Jñāna/Jñā<u>n</u>am: Knowledge/wisdom

Kavi Pāṭṭu: A kind of ritual singing specific to Alvar Tirunagari

Kayal: A freshwater fish native to Tamil country

Kālamayakkam: Literally, the bewilderment of the seasons. It generally refers to a deliberate misapprehension of the signs of the approaching rainy season.

Kāma: The god of love

Keṇṭai: A freshwater fish native to Tamil country

Kiḷavi-t-talaivan̲: The hero of the poem/the moment(s)

Kon̲r̲ai: Indian laburnum

Kōvai: A genre of Tamil poetry. It usually contains four hundred verses, and is concerned with depicting all the stages of love, beginning with the first meeting and concluding with life after marriage

Kurukūr: The town identified with present-day Alvar Tirunagari in Tirunelveli, Tamil Nadu

Kur̲ai: Lack

Kuvaḷai: Blue water lily

Kūrattāl̲vān̲: Rāmānuja's* scribe and disciple

Lakṣmī: Viṣṇu's primary consort. She is the goddess of wealth, fortune and auspiciousness.

Līlā vibhūti: The realm of play. It refers to the terrestrial world.

Mahābali: The demon king vanquished by Viṣṇu in his Vāmana-Trivikrama form

Maṇipravāḷa: Literally, gems and corals. It refers to a commentarial language used by the Śrīvaiṣṇavas.* It uses specialized Sanskrit vocabulary with Tamil grammar.

Maturakavi: The disciple of Nammāl̲vār*

Māṇikkavācakar: A ninth-century Śaiva poet

Mārkal̲i: The Tamil month that falls between mid-December and mid-January

Mār̲an̲: A name or epithet of Nammāl̲vār*

Māruta: A type of cool breeze

Meru: The mountain that is the cosmic axis mundi

Mokṣa: Release from the endless cycle of birth and death

Murukaṉ: The Tamil god of love and war. He is the son of Śiva.

Naraka: An asura* who kidnapped several women and was eventually killed by Kṛṣṇa

Nācciyār Tirumoḻi: A poem of 143 verses composed by Āṇṭāḷ*

Nālāyira Divya Prabandham (also, *Divya Prabandham*): A collection of four thousand verses composed by the twelve āḻvār* poets

Nammāḻvār: The most important of the āḻvār* poets

Nāthamuni: The first teacher of the Śrīvaiṣṇava* community. He is believed to have collected and compiled the *Divya Prabandham*.*

Nāyaka(ṉ): (Sanskrit) Hero

Nāyikā: (Sanskrit) Heroine

Neytal: Indian water lily

Nityasūri: Eternal being

Nitya vibhūti: Eternal realm. Refers to Vaikuṇṭha*

Oppu: Comparison

Paṇ: An ancient Tamil musical mode

Parāṅkuśa Nāyikā: Nammāḻvār's* female persona

Pāṭṭuṭai-t-talaivaṉ: The hero of the composition/patron

Periyāḻvār: An important āḻvār,* who is related to Āṇṭāḷ*

Periyavāccāṉ Piḷḷai: A twelfth-century commentator on the *Nālāyira Divya Prabandham**

Pēriṉpam: The higher pleasure, that is, divine bliss

Pēy: One of the first three āḻvār*

Phala śruti: The concluding verse of a poem detailing the merits to be accrued from learning, memorizing or reciting it

Poykai: One of the first three āḻvār*

Puṟam: Literally, exterior/outer. It refers to the category of Tamil classical poems that deals with kings, war and ethics.

Puṟanāṉuṟu: A Tamil literary anthology of four hundred verses from the classical period that concerns war and ethics

Pūtam: One of the first three āḻvār*

Rāga: A melodic mode

Rāmānuja: The most important of the teachers of the Śrivaiṣṇava* community. The traditional dates are 1017–1137 CE.

Rāmānuja Nūṟṟantāti: A text in praise of Rāmānuja

Ṛg Veda: The oldest of the four Vedas. Considered to be revealed or *śruti* (heard)

Saṁpradāya: Tradition, lineage

Saṁsāra: The endless cycle of birth and death

Saṁśleṣa: Union

Śaṭhakōpaṉ: One of Nammāḻvār's* names

Śleṣa: A literary device that allows you to say many things at once. Yigal Bronner refers to it as 'simultaneous narration'.

Śrī: Another name for Lakṣmī, the primary consort of Viṣṇu

Śrīvaiṣṇava: A sect that reveres the āḻvārs* and cleaves to the philosophy laid out by Rāmānuja*

Svāpadeśa: The inner/esoteric meaning

Talaivaṉ: (Tamil) Hero

Talaivi: (Tamil) Heroine

Tāla: Rhythm

Tēvāram: The Śaiva collection of poems attributed to the three saints Appar, Campantar and Cuntarar

Tillai: The sacred site of Chidambaram and home to Śiva as Naṭarāja, the king of dance

Tiṇai: Landscapes. It refers to a Tamil poetic system. There are five *tiṇais*, each of which is associated with a specific moment in the development of love. These are *kuṟiñci*, *neytal*, *pālai*, *mullai* and *marutam*.

Tirukkōvaiyār: The four-hundred-verse poem in the *kōvai** genre composed by Māṇikkavācakar*

Tirumaṅkai: One of the most important āḻvār* poets with an impressive contribution of poems to the *Divya Prabandham**

Tirumoḻi: A type of song favoured by the āḻvār* poets

Tiruppāvai: The Sacred Vow. Āṇṭāḷ's* composition of thirty verses in praise of Kṛṣṇa

Tiruvācakam: Literally, sacred speech. Māṇikkavācakar's* monumental work in praise of Śiva

Tiruvāymoḻi: Literally, sacred truth. Nammāḻvār's* 1102-verse composition. The Śrīvaiṣṇavas regarded it as revealed.

Tolkāppiyam: A Tamil grammar which has several layers. The earliest strata of the text is generally dated to the pre-Christian era (c. 150 BCE) with the upper limit for the text's composition placed at 500 CE.

Tōḻi: (Tamil) The female friend

Tuḻāy/Tulasī: Sacred basil

Vaikuṇṭha: Viṣṇu's heaven

Vedānta Deśika: One of the most important teachers, poets and philosophers of the Śrīvaiṣṇava* community. He composed in Sanskrit, Tamil and Prakrit. He lived between 1269 and 1370 CE. His work and philosophical orientation comes to be associated with the northern or Vaṭakalai branch of the Śrīvaiṣṇavas.

Vēlan̲: The priest of Murukan̲.* In Caṅkam poems he is often painted as an ineffectual figure who misdiagnoses the heroine's lovesickness as possession by Murukan̲.

Vēḷḷāḷa: An agricultural caste group

Viṇṇappam: Petition, plea or request

Vin̲ai: Deeds or actions

Viruttam: A specific metrical form

Viśleṣa: Separation

Viśvaksena: Viṣṇu's commander-in-chief/guard

BIBLIOGRAPHY

Primary Sources

Aṇṇaṅkarācarya, P.B. *Ālvārkal Talaivarāṉa Nammāḻvār Aruḷicceyta Mutaṟ Pirapantamākiya Tiruviruttam*. Chennai: Māṭal Accukkūṭam, 1930.

Aṉṉapukaḻ Muṭumpai Aḻakiya Maṇavāḷa Perumāḷ Nāyaṉār Aruḷicceyta. *Ācārya Hṛdayam*. Madras: Madras Rattiṉam Press, 1950.

Divyasūricaritam. Garuḍavāhana Paṇḍita. Sanskrit text. Eds. T.A. Sampath Kumaracharya and K.K.A.Venkatachari. Bombay: Ananthacharya Research Institute, 1978.

Guruparamparaprabhāvam 6000. Maṇipravāḷa text. Eds. Srinivasa Appankarswami et al. Chennai: Ganesh Publications. Publication date unavailable.

Guruparamparaprābhavam 3000. Maṇipravāḷa text. Tiruvallikkēṉi: Sri Vanibhusanam Publishers, 1913.

Nālāyira Divya Prabandham. Tamil text. Ed. P.B. Aṇṇaṅkarācarya. Kanci: Aṇṇaṅkarācarya Institute, 1972.

Nālāyira Divya Prabandham. Tamil text. Ed. Krishnaswami Iyengar. Trichy: Srinivasa Press. Publication date unavailable.

Periyavāccan̲ Piḷḷai. *Tiruviruttam Vyākhyān̲am*. Kodambakkam, Chennai: Sri Vaishava Sri, 1994.

Rāmānujāccāryār Caṭakōpa U.Vē Vai Mu. *Prapantajanakūṭastar Śrī Nammāḻvār Tiruvāy Malarntaruḷiya Tiruviruttam Urai*. 3rd edn. Chennai: Sri Vaishnava Sri, 1994.

Vīrarāghavācarya, Uttamūr T. *Ubhaya Vedānta Granthamālai: Nammāḻvār Aruḷicceyta Tiruviruttam, Tiruvāciriyam, Periya Tiruvantāti*. Madras: Visishtadvaita Pracharini Sabha, 1954.

Secondary Sources

Aiyangar, Krishnaswami S. *Early History of Vaishnavism in South India*. Oxford: Oxford University Press, 1920.

Bard, Amy. '"No Power of Speech Remains": Tears and Transformation in South Asian *Majlis* Poetry.' *Holy Tears: Weeping in the Religious Imagination*. Princeton, N.J.: Princeton University Press, 2005. Pp. 145–64.

Bharati, Srirama. *The Sacred Book of Four Thousand: Nalayira Divya Prabandham Rendered in English with Tamil Original*. Chennai: Sri Sadagopan Tirunarayanaswami Divya Prabandha Pathasala, 2000.

Bronner, Yigal. *Extreme Poetry: The South Asian Movement of Simultaneous Narration*. New York: Oxford University Press, 2010.

Carman, John. 'Dissolving One Paradox and Discovering Another: Pillan's Interpretation of Nammalvar's Poem.' *Religion and Public Culture: Encounters and Identities in Modern South India*. Richmond, Surrey: Curzon Press, 2000. Pp. 149–61.

Carman, John and Vasudha Narayanan. *The Tamil Veda: Piḷḷān̲'s Interpretation of the Tiruvāymoḻi*. Chicago and London: University of Chicago Press, 1989.

Chari, S.M.S. *Philosophy and Theistic Mysticism of the Āḻvārs*. Delhi: Motilal Banarasidass, 1997.

Clark-Decès, Isabelle. *The Encounter Never Ends: A Return to the Field of Tamil Rituals*. Albany: State University of New York Press, 2007.

———. *No One Cries for the Dead: Tamil Dirges, Rowdy Songs and Graveyard Petitions*. Berkeley: University of California Press, 2005.

Clooney, Francis X, S.J. '"I Created Land and Sea": A Tamil Case of God-Consciousness and Its Śrīvaiṣṇava Interpretation.' *Numen*, Vol. 35, Fasc. 2 (December 1988), pp. 238–59.

———. 'Nammāḻvār's Glorious Tiruvallavāḻ: An Exploration in the Methods and Goals of Śrīvaiṣṇava Commentary.' *Journal of the American Oriental Society*, Vol. 111, No. 2 (April–June 1991), pp. 260–76.

———. *Seeing through Texts: Doing Theology among the Śrīvaiṣṇavas of South India*. Albany: State University of New York, 1996.

Clooney, Francis X, S.J., and Archana Venkatesan. Trans. *Tiruvāymoḻi*. Penguin Classics. Forthcoming.

Cutler, Norman. *Consider Our Vow: Translation of Tiruppāvai and Tiruvempāvai into English*. Madurai: Muttu Patippakam, 1979.

———. 'Four Spatial Realms in *Tirukkōvaiyār*.' *Tamil Geographies: Cultural Constructions of Space and Place in South India*. Albany: State University of New York Press, 2008. Pp. 43–57.

———. *Songs of Experience: The Poetics of Tamil Devotion*. Bloomington and Indianapolis: Indiana University Press, 1987.

Damodaran, G. *Ācārya Hṛdayam: A Critical Study*. Tirupati: Tirumalai Tirupati Devasthanams, 1976.

Dehejia, Vidya. *Slaves of the Lord: Path of the Tamiḻ Saints*. 1st edn. South Asia Books, 2002.

Egnor, Margaret T. 'Internal Iconicity in Paraiyars' "Crying Songs".' *Another Harmony: New Essays on the Folklore of India*. Eds. Stuart H. Blackburn and A.K. Ramanujan. Berkeley: University of California Press, 1986. Pp. 294–344.

Govindacharya, Alkondavilli. *The Divine Wisdom of the Drâvida Saints*. Madras: C.N. Press, 1902.

———. *The Holy Lives of the Azhvars or the Dravida Saints*. Bombay: Ananthacharya Indological Research Institute, 1982.

Graham, Carol. 'The Inauguration of the Church of South India.' *The International Review of Missions*. Eds. Norman Goodall and Margaret Sinclair. Vol. 37 (1948), pp. 49–53.

Handelman, Don, and David Shulman. *Siva in the Forest of Pines: An Essay on Sorcery and Self-Knowledge*. New Delhi: Oxford University Press, 2004.

Hardy, Friedhelm. 'The Formation of Srivaisnavism.' *Charisma and Canon: Essays on the Religious History of the Indian Subcontinent*. Eds. Vasudha Dalmia, Angelika Malinar and Martin Christof. New Delhi: Oxford University Press, 2001. Pp. 41–61.

———. 'A Radical Reassessment of the Vedic Heritage—the *Ācāryahṛdayam* and Its Wider Implications.' *Representing Hinduism: The Construction of Religious Traditions and National Identity*. Eds. Vasudha Dalmia and Heinrich von Stietencron. New Delhi: Sage Publications, 1995. Pp. 35–50.

———. 'The ŚrīVaiṣṇava Hagiography of Parakāla.' *Indian Narrative: Perspectives and Patterns*. Eds. Christopher Shackle and Rupert Snell. Wiesbaden: Otto Harrassowitz, 1992. Pp. 81–116.

———. 'The Tamil Veda of a Śūdra Saint: The Śrīvaiṣṇava Interpretation of Nammāḻvār.' *Contributions to South Asian Studies I*. Delhi: Oxford University Press, 1979. Pp. 29–87.

———. *Viraha-Bhakti: The Early History of Kṛṣṇa Devotion in South India*. New Delhi: Oxford University Press, 1983.

Hart, George L. *The Poems of Ancient Tamil: Their Milieu and Their Sanskrit Counterparts*. Berkeley: University of California Press, 1988.

———. *Poets of the Tamil Anthologies: Ancient Poems of Love and War*. Princeton, N.J: Princeton University Press, 1979.

Hancock, Mary. 'The Dilemmas of Domesticity: Possession and Devotional Experience among Urban Smārta Women.' *From the Margins of Hindu Marriage*. Eds. Lindsey Harlan and Paul B. Courtright. New York: Oxford University Press, 1995. Pp. 60–91.

Hawley, John Stratton. 'Author and Authority in the Bhakti Poetry of North India.' *The Journal of Asian Studies*, Vol. 47, No. 2 (May 1988), pp. 269–290.

———. 'The *Gopīs'* Tears.' *Holy Tears: Weeping in the Religious Imagination*. Princeton, N.J.: Princeton University Press, 2005. Pp. 94–111.

———. *The Memory of Love: Sūrdās Sings to Krishna*. New York: Oxford University Press, 2009.

Hooper, J.S.M. *The Bible in India with a Chapter on Ceylon*. London: Oxford University Press, 1938.

———. *Bible Translation in India, Pakistan and Ceylon*. Bombay: Oxford University Press, 1963.

———. *Hymns of the Ālvārs*. Calcutta: Association Press; Oxford: Oxford University Press, 1929.

Hopkins, Steven P. 'Extravagant Beholding: Love, Ideal Bodies and Particularity.' *History of Religions*, Vol. 47, No. 1 (August 2007), pp. 1–50.

———. '"I Walk Weeping in Pangs of a Mother's Torment for Her Children." Women's Laments in the Poetry and Prophecies of William Blake.' *Journal of Religious Ethics*, Vol. 37, No. 1 (2009), pp. 39–81.

———. *An Ornament for Jewels: Love Poems for the Lord of Gods by Vedāntadeśika*. New York: Oxford University Press, 2007.

———. *Singing the Body of God: The Hymns of Vedāntadeśika in Their South Indian Tradition*. New Delhi: Oxford University Press, 2002.

Jagadeesan, N. *Collected Papers on Tamil Vaishnavism*. Madurai: New Rathna Press, 1989.

———. *History of Sri Vaishnavism in the Tamil Country (Post-Ramanuja)*. Madurai: Koodal Publishers, 1977.

Jeyarajan, Ḳokkalai. *Nammāḻvār Aruḷiya Tiruviruttam: Oru Tiṟaṉāyvu*. Chennai: Maharani Publications, 1997.

Kingsbury, F., and G.E. Phillips. *Hymns of the Tamil Śaivite Saints*. London: Oxford University Press, 1921.

Krishnaswami, K.R. *Iyarpa: 4000 Divya Prabandham Series*. Vol. 8. Bangalore: A&K Prakashana, 2010.

Mumme, Patricia. 'Śrīvaiṣṇava Hagiography: Lessons from Biblical Scholarship.' *Journal of Vaiṣṇava Studies*, Vol. 5, No. 2 (Spring 1997), pp. 157–84.

Nabokov, Isabelle. *Religion against the Self: An Ethnography of Tamil Rituals*. New York: Oxford University Press, 2000.

Nandakumar, Prema. *Nammalvar's 'Tiruviruttam': The Drama of the Love Divine*. Calcutta: Writers' Workshop Publications, 1979.

Narayanan, Vasudha. 'The Realm of Play and the Sacred Stage.' *Gods at Play: Līlā in South Asia*. Ed. William Sax. New York: Oxford University Press, 1995. Pp. 177–204.

———. *The Vernacular Veda: Revelation, Recitation and Ritual*. Columbia, S.C.: University of South Carolina Press, 1994.

———. *The Way and the Goal: Expressions of Devotion in the Early Śrī Vaiṣṇava Tradition*. Washington, D.C.: Institute for Vaishnava Studies and Center for the Study of World Religions, Harvard University, 1987.

———. '"With the Earth as a Lamp and the Sun as the Flame": Lighting Devotion in South India.' *International Journal of Hindu Studies*, Vol. 11, No. 3 (December 2007), pp. 227–53.

Newbigin, Lesslie, J.E. 'The Reunion of the Church: A Defence of the South India Scheme.' Revised edn. London: SCM Press, 1960.

Pandian, Anand. *Crooked Stalks: Cultivating Virtue in South India*. Durham, N.C.: Duke University Press, 2009.

Parthasarathy, R. trans. *The Tale of an Anklet, An Epic of South India: The Cilappatikāram of Ilaṅkō Aṭikaḷ*. New York: Columbia University Press, 1992.

Patton, Kimberly Christine, and John Stratton Hawley. 'Introduction.' *Holy Tears: Weeping in the Religious Imagination*. Princeton, N.J.: Princeton University Press, 2005. Pp. 1–23.

Pillai, Vaiyapuri. *History of Tamil Language and Literature: Beginning to 1000 AD*. Madras: New Century Book House, 1956.

Peterson, Indira Viswanathan. *Poems to Śiva: The Hymns of the Tamil Saints*. Delhi: Motilal Banarasidass Publishers, 1991.

Proceedings of the 10th Annual Meeting of the National Christian Council of India, Burma and Ceylon. 26–29 November 1946. Nelson Square, Nagpur: Office of the National Christian Council.

Proceedings of the 5th Meeting of the National Christian Council, Nagpur. 31 December 1932–4 January 1933. Nelson Square, Nagpur: Office of the National Christian Council.

Raghavan, V. 'The Name Pāñcarātra: With an Analysis of the Sanatkumāra-Saṁhitā in Manuscript.' *Journal of the American Oriental Society*, Vol. 85, No. 1 (January–March 1965), pp.73–79.

Ramanujan, A.K. *Hymns for the Drowning: Poems for Viṣṇu by Nammāḻvār*. Princeton, N.J.: Princeton University Press, 1981.

———. *The Interior Landscape: Love Poems from a Classical Tamil Anthology*. New Delhi: Oxford University Press, 1994.

———. 'Is There an Indian Way of Thinking?' *The Collected Essays of A.K. Ramanujan*. Ed. Vinay Dharwadker. New Delhi: Oxford University Press, 1999. Pp. 34–51.

———. 'Men, Women, and Saints.' *The Collected Essays of A.K. Ramanujan*. Ed. Vinay Dharwadker. New Delhi: Oxford University Press, 1999. Pp. 279–94.

———. 'On Translating a Tamil Poem.' *The Collected Essays of A.K. Ramanujan*. Ed. Vinay Dharwadker. New Delhi: Oxford University Press, 1999. Pp. 219–31.

———. 'Towards an Anthology of City Images.' *The Collected Essays of A.K. Ramanujan*. Ed. Vinay Dharwadker. New Delhi: Oxford University Press, 1999. Pp. 52–72.

———. 'Where Mirrors Are Windows: Towards an Anthology of Reflections.' *History of Religions*, Vol. 28, No. 3 (1989), pp. 187–216.

Ramanujan, A.K., and Norman Cutler. 'From Classicism to *Bhakti*.' *The Collected Essays of A.K. Ramanujan*. Ed. Vinay Dharwadker. New Delhi: Oxford University Press, 1999. Pp. 232–59.

Ramanujam, B.V. *History of Vaishnavism in South India upto Ramanuja*. Chidambaram: Annamalai University Press, 1973.

Rao, Gopinatha T.A. *Sir Subrahmanya Ayyar Lectures on the History of the Śrī Vaiṣṇavas*. Madras: Government Press, 1923.

Reddiyar, Venkatacami, K. *Śrī Nammāḻvār Aruḷicceyta Tiruviruttam*. Srirangam: Srirangam Srimat Andavan Asramam, 1984.

Renganathan, Vasu. 'The Element of Beauty and the Use of Similes in Tamil Poetics.' Paper delivered at the 8th Annual Tamil Conference, UC Berkeley, 21 April 2012.

Richards, F.J. Review of *The Heritage of India Series: Hymns of the Āḻvārs* by J.S.M. Hooper. *Journal of the Royal Asiatic Society of Great Britain and Ireland*, No. 3 (July 1934), pp. 590–92.

Sastri, Nilakantha K.A. *Development of Religion in South India*. Madras: Orient Longman, 1963.

———. *A History of South India: From Prehistoric Times to the Fall of Vijayanagar*. 3rd edn. Madras: Oxford University Press, 1966.

Selby, Martha Ann. 'Dialogues of Space, Desires, and Gender in Tamil *Caṅkam* Poetry.' *Tamil Geographies: Cultural Constructions of Space and Place in South India*. Albany: State University of New York Press, 2008. Pp. 17–42.

———. *Grow Long Blessed Night: Love Poems from Classical India*. New York: Oxford University Press, 2000.

———. *Tamil Love Poetry: The Five Hundred Short Poems of the Aiṅkuṟunūṟu*. New York: Columbia University Press, 2011.

Sethuraman, N. *The Imperial Pandyas: Mathematics Reconstructs the Chronology*. Kumbakonam: Raman and Raman Private Limited, 1978.

———. *The Later Pandyas* (1371–1759 AD). Paper presented at the 19th Annual Congress of the Epigraphical Society of India, 12–14 February 1993. Tiruchirappalli: Bharatidasan University.

———. *Medieval Pandyas* (AD 1000–1200). Kumbakonam: Raman and Raman Private Limited, 1980.

Sharpe, Eric J. *Not to Destroy but to Fulfil: The Contribution of J.N. Farquhar to Protestant Missionary Thought in India before 1914*. Uppsala: Swedish Institute of Missionary Research, 1965.

Shulman, David. 'Embracing the Subject: Harṣa's Play within a Play.' *Journal of Indian Philosophy*, Vol. 25 (1997), pp. 69–89.

———. 'On Being Human in the Sanskrit Epic: The Riddle of Nala.' *Journal of Indian Philosophy*, Vol. 22 (1994), pp. 1–29.

———. '*Tirukkovaiyār*: Downstream into God.' *Self and Self-Transformation in the History of Religions*. Eds. David Shulman and Guy G. Stroumsa. New York: Oxford University Press, 2002. Pp. 131–49.

———. 'The Yogi's Human Self: Tāyumāṉavar in the Tamil Mystical Tradition.' *Religion*, Vol. 21 (1991), pp. 51–72.

Smith, Frederick M. *The Self Possessed: Deity and Spirit Possession in South Asian Literature and Civilization*. New York: Columbia University Press, 2006.

Stein, Burton. *Peasant State and Society in Medieval South India*. Delhi: Oxford University Press, 1980.

Sundkler, Bengt. *Church of South India: The Movement towards Union, 1900–1947*. London: Lutterworth Press, 1954.

Takahashi, Takanobu. *Poetry and Poetics: Literary Conventions of Tamil Love Poetry*. PhD dissertation. University of Utrecht, 1989.

Trawick, Margaret. 'Ambiguity in the Oral Exegesis of a Sacred Text: Tirukkōvaiyār (Or, the Guru in the Garden, Being an Account of a Tamil Informant's Responses to Homesteading in Central New York State).' *Cultural Anthropology*, Vol. 3, No. 3 (August 1988), pp. 316–51.

———. *Notes on Love in a Tamil Family*. Berkeley: University of California Press, 1992.

———. 'Spirits and Voices in Tamil Songs.' *American Ethnologist*, Vol. 15, No. 2 (May 1989), pp. 193–215.

van Buitenen, J.A.B. 'Pāñcarātra.' *History of Religions*, Vol. 1, No. 2 (Winter 1962), pp. 291–99.

Venkatachari, K.K.A. 'Abhayapradānasāra.' *Journal of the Oriental Institute*, Vol. XLVIII, Nos. 1–4 (1998–1999), pp. 201–12.

———. *The Maṇipravāḷa Literature of the Śrīvaiṣṇavaācārya-s*. Bombay: Ananthacharya Institute, 1978.

Venkatesan, Archana. *Āṇṭāḷ and Her Magic Mirror: Her Life as a Poet in the Guises of the Goddess*. PhD dissertation. University of California, Berkeley, 2004.

———. 'A Different Kind of Āṇṭāḷ Story: The *Divyasūricaritam* of Garuḍavāhana Paṇḍita.' *Journal of Hindu Studies*, Vol. 6, No. 3 (November 2013), pp. 243–96.

———. 'Double the Pleasure: Reading Nammāḻvār's *Tiruviruttam*.' *Passages: Relationships between Tamil and Sanskrit*. Eds. M. Kannan and Jennifer Clare. Pondicherry: French Institute of Pondicherry, 2009. Pp. 267–79.

———. 'The Poet's Song: Maturakavi and Nammāḻvār in Performance at the Alvar Tirunagari Temple.' Forthcoming.

———. *The Secret Garland: Āṇṭāḷ's Tiruppāvai and Nācciyār Tirumoḻi*. New York: Oxford University Press, 2010.

———. 'A Woman's Kind of Love: Female Longing in Tamil Alvar Poetry.' *Journal of Hindu Christian Studies*, Vol. 20 (2007), pp. 16–24.

Venugopal, I.P. *Nammāḻvār Tiruviruttamum Māṇikkavācakar Tirukkōvaiyārum*. Vellore: Sukuntalā Veḷiyiṭṭakam, 1992.

Wainwright, Geoffrey. *Lesslie Newbigin: A Theological Life*. New York: Oxford University Press, 2000.

Wilden, Eva. *Kuṟuntokai: A Critical Edition and an Annotated Translation of the Kuṟuntokai* (Vol. 1). Pondicherry: École Française d'Extrême-Orient and Tamiḻmaṇ Patippakam, 2010.

Yocum, Glenn E. 'Shrines, Shamanism, and Love Poetry: Elements in the Emergence of Popular Tamil Bhakti.' *Journal of the American Academy of Religion*, Vol. 41, No. 1 (March 1973), pp. 3–17.

Young, Katherine. *Beloved Places: The Correlation of Topography and Theology in the Śrīvaiṣṇava Tradition of South India*. PhD dissertation. McGill University, 1978.

Younger, Paul. 'Singing the Tamil Hymn Book in the Tradition of Rāmānuja: The Adyayanotsava Festival in Srirangam.' *History of Religions*, Vol. 21, No. 3 (1982), pp. 272–93.

Zvelebil, Kamil. *Companion Studies to the History of Tamil Literature*. Leiden: E.J. Brill, 1992.

Zvelebil, Kamil. *Tamil Literature*. Leiden: E.J. Brill, 1975.

Zvelebil, Kamil. *A History of Indian Literature: Tamil Literature*. Wiesbaden: Otto Harrassowitz, 1974.

Zvelebil, Kamil. *The Smile of Murugan: On Tamil Literature of South India*. Leiden: E.J. Brill, 1973.

Electronic Sources

Bharati, Srirama. araiyar.com. Last accessed 7 February 2013.

Nagaswamy, R. 'A New Pandya Record and the Dates of Nayanmars and Alvars'. http://tamilartsacademy.com/articles/article08.xml. Last accessed 19 January 2013.

Oppiliappan Koil Sri Varadachari Sathakopan. *Thiruviruttham and Rg Vedam*. http://www.sadagopan.org/index.php/categories/doc_details/241-ss083-thiruviruttham-synopsis. Last accessed 5 February 2013.

YOU MAY ALSO LIKE

Hymns for the Drowning
Nammalvar

Translated by A.K. Ramanujan

'It was Ramanujan's translations that first made it possible for the non-Sanskrit literatures of India to stake their claim at the canonical altar'—*Caravan*

The poems in this book are some of the earliest about Visnu, one of the Hindu Trinity, also known as Tirumal, the Dark One. Tradition recognizes twelve alvars, saint-poets devoted to Visnu, who lived between the sixth and ninth century in the Tamil-speaking region of south India. These devotees of Visnu and their counterparts, the devotees of Siva (nayanmar), changed and revitalized Hinduism, and their devotional hymns addressed to Visnu are among the earliest bhakti (devotional) texts in any Indian language. In this selection from Nammalvar's works, the translations like the originals reflect the alternations of philosophic hymns and love poems, through recurring voices, roles and places. They also enact a progression from wonder at the Lord's works to the experience of loving him and watching others love him, to moods of questioning and despair and finally to the experience of being devoured and possessed by him.

Penguin Classics/PB

I, Lalla: The Poems of Lal Dĕd

Translated by Ranjit Hoskote

Winner of the Sahitya Akademi Award

The poems of the fourteenth-century Kashmiri mystic Lal Dĕd, popularly known as Lalla, strike us like brief and blinding bursts of light. Emotionally rich yet philosophically precise, sumptuously enigmatic yet crisply structured, these poems are as sensuously evocative as they are charged with an ecstatic devotion. Stripping away a century of Victorian-inflected translations and paraphrases, and restoring the jagged, colloquial power of Lalla's voice, in Ranjit Hoskote's new translation these poems are glorious manifestos of illumination.

'Hoskote's translations are unadorned and distilled down to the essence . . . Lal Ded's poetry is as timeless and as perfect as the beauty of Kashmir. It reflects the latent yearnings that exist in all seekers'—
Times of India, Crest edition

Penguin Classics/PB

Kabir: The Weaver's Song

Translated by Vinay Dharwadker

Winner of the Sahitya Akademi Award

'Knowledge ahead, knowledge behind, knowledge to the left and right. The knowledge that knows what knowledge is: that's the knowledge that's mine'—Bijak, Sakhi 188

One of India's greatest mystics, Kabir (1398–1448) was also a satirist and philosopher, a poet of timeless wit and wisdom. Equally immersed in theology and social thought, music and politics, his songs have won devoted followers from every walk of life through the past five centuries. He was a Muslim by name, but his ideas stand at the intersection of Hinduism and Islam, Bhakti and Yoga, religion and secularism. And his words were always marked by rhetorical boldness and conceptual subtlety.

This book offers Vinay Dharwadker's sparkling new translations of one hundred poems, drawing for the first time on major sources in half a dozen literary languages. They closely mimic the structure, voice and style of the originals, revealing Kabir's multiple facets in historical and cultural contexts. Finely balancing simplicity and complexity, this selection opens up new forms of imagination and experience for discerning readers around the world.

Penguin Classics/PB